Naturally Supernatural

Chad Gonzales

Auxano Publications

Naturally Supernatural

ISBN 13: 978-0-9853392-7-2

Copyright © 2015 by Chad W. Gonzales

TABLE OF CONTENTS

Introduction

After I graduated from Bible school, Lacy and I married and moved to Beaumont, Texas where I grew up as a child. Even though I was presented with several ministry opportunities after Bible school, I sensed we were to go back and volunteer in the church where I had grown up. I knew we were to start a church, but I also knew the time was not right then, so for the next three years, I simply continued to prepare myself for the next phase of ministry.

It was during this time God began to create such a stirring within me for the supernatural. I began to study the subject of our union with Christ and began to see things in a light I had never seen before. When we launched our church in College Station, TX, we put a major focus on the supernatural. I was desirous for it and God met our faith.

We began to experience the miraculous on a level I had never experienced before. Our third month in a blind lady was healed. A few weeks later, three tumors dissolved on a little boy's head and he was completely healed of Hodgkin's disease. Things just continued to snowball until within a two year time, we had over twenty cancers healed. Lacy and I were seeing short limbs growing out, damaged nerves mended, deaf ears healed and lots more on a regular basis.

During this time of experiencing miracles, I began to grow in my understanding of things; of course, when you are venturing out in an area you don't know much about, not only do you get answers, but you also acquire more questions. When I have had questions about walking in the supernatural, I go to Jesus. I began to study the Gospels like I had never done before, especially the Gospel of John. I wanted to see not just what Jesus did, but why and how Jesus did what He did.

I'll never forget one day as I was studying the ministry of Jesus, the Holy Spirit spoke to me. I'm not saying I heard an audible voice, but on the inside, very clearly I heard these words, "Jesus was naturally supernatural." This statement caused me to start looking at Jesus from a different perspective and how He did what He did. I noticed that Jesus wasn't always in the temple when the supernatural was happening in his life; the vast majority of the time, it was in the wilderness, in the streets, in the marketplace and in homes. Jesus would be simply walking down the road, enjoying a wedding, or sitting by a well and the supernatural would happen.

I began to see John 14:12 from a different perspective in which Jesus said, "The same works you saw Me do, you will do also and even greater works." At that point, I became not only inspired, but excited; I wanted to experience in my life what Jesus experienced – not only for me but for others.

Occasionally, Christians get a taste of the supernatural, but rarely know why. Experiencing the supernatural for the majority of Christians happens more on accident than on purpose! This shouldn't be the case. When we accepted Jesus as our Lord and Savior, He eliminated the limits. How far we go in the things of God is completely up to us. It's not up to God, Jesus, the Holy Spirit and certainly not the devil; it is absolutely up to us.

I want to introduce you to a life of the supernatural that is lived on purpose and lived without formulas. I want to introduce you to the life God intended for His people before the very foundation of the world. It's God's plan and His desire that you and I live a life that is naturally supernatural.

Chad Gonzales

June 2015

Chapter 1
A Supernatural Beginning

If you look at Christianity, there are a lot of us living with boundaries. The reason we are living with boundaries and not living the life God originally planned for us is because we don't really understand what happened when we received salvation. We have a good understanding that when we were saved, there was a change in our eternity, so we get to go to Heaven; although, beyond going to Heaven, we haven't dared to fully grasp the change that happened in our now.

17 This means that anyone who belongs to Christ has become a new person. The old life is gone; a new life has begun!

2 Corinthians 5:17 NLT

17 Therefore if any person is [ingrafted] in Christ (the Messiah) he is a new creation (a new creature altogether); the old [previous moral and spiritual condition] has passed away. Behold, the fresh and new has come!

2 Corinthians 5:17 AMP

When we accepted Jesus as our Lord and Savior, we became a brand new creature that never existed before; obviously, this is referring to our spirit man. Nothing changed on the outside, but something certainly changed on the inside when you were born again. When you accepted Jesus, if you were tall before, you were tall after; if you had blue eyes before, you had blue eyes after. It wasn't your body that became brand new, but it was your spirit man that became brand new because you were born again.

A Supernatural Birth Place

1 There was a man named Nicodemus, a Jewish religious leader who was a Pharisee. 2 After dark one evening, he came to speak with Jesus. "Rabbi," he said, "we all know that God has sent you to teach us.

Your miraculous signs are evidence that God is with you." 3 Jesus replied, "I tell you the truth, unless you are born again, you cannot see the Kingdom of God." 4 "What do you mean?" exclaimed Nicodemus. "How can an old man go back into his mother's womb and be born again?"5 Jesus replied, "I assure you, no one can enter the Kingdom of God without being born of water and the Spirit. 6 Humans can reproduce only human life, but the Holy Spirit gives birth to spiritual life. 7 So don't be surprised when I say, 'You must be born again.' 8 The wind blows wherever it wants. Just as you can hear the wind but can't tell where it comes from or where it is going, so you can't explain how people are born of the Spirit."

John 3:1-8 NLT

In John 3, we find the story of Nicodemus having a secret meeting with Jesus. In this conversation, Jesus states the necessity of being born again. Jesus said that in order to see and experience the kingdom of God, you had to be born again. The literal Greek of verse 4 says, "...you must be born from above." So when we are born again, we are literally born in Heaven.

When you were born from your mother, you were

probably born in a hospital; when you were born from God, you were born in Heaven! Heaven is your citizenship! Heaven is your birthplace! You are literally from another planet. Some people ask me if I believe in aliens and my response is always "Yes!" When they ask why I believe in aliens, I tell them I believe in them because I am one! I am from another world called Heaven and it is my home. (For further study of this wonderful truth, read my book ALIENS.)

One of my favorite passages of Scripture is John 17. Here we find Jesus praying in the Garden of Gethsemane and in His prayer, we discover marvelous truths regarding our identity.

> **14 I have given them Your word; and the world has hated them because they are not of the world, just as I am not of the world. 15 I do not pray that You should take them out of the world, but that You should keep them from the evil one. 16 They are not of the world, just as I am not of the world.**
>
> **John 17:14-16 NKJV**

Jesus said He was not of this world and then went on to say that in the very same way, in the very same manner, to the very same degree, we are not of this world either! The supernatural should be natural to us; it should be normal for us because it is who we are. There is a saying in Texas that you can take the man out of Texas but you can't take Texas out of the man. Well, the same thing is vitally true in a spiritual sense. You can take the man out of Heaven, but you can't take Heaven out of the man. When I was born again, I was birthed out of Heaven. I may not be in Heaven right now, but there is some Heaven inside of me – it's called the life of God!

The reason this is so important for you is because you need to realize your very birth was supernatural; your beginning was supernatural! Now if your beginning was supernatural and initiated by God, why would you think the rest of your existence would be destined by God to be any less supernatural?

A Supernatural Heritage

Not only were you born from a supernatural place, you were born from a supernatural Father! 1 Peter 1:23 tells us we were born of incorruptible seed. The word *incorruptible* comes from the Greek word *Aphthartos* which means immortal, imperishable and not subject to decay.[1] So, we can readily see that this isn't talking about our human body; no, this is talking about our spirit man that was birthed from the seed of God. In other words, you partook of God's very own life and nature; you got God's DNA!

7 And the Lord God formed man of the dust of the ground and breathed into his nostrils the breath of life; and man became a living being.

Genesis 2:7 NKJV

God breathed into man Himself. The literal Hebrew of this verse states that man became a speaking spirit.[2] What we see here in Creation was God's original plan. Because Adam chose to sell out to Satan, man lost not only his fellowship with God, but also His union with God. Thankfully, Jesus loved us enough that He came to restore man back to his original place.

This is why Jesus said to Nicodemus in John 3:5 that we had to be born again. Because of what Adam did, we were naturally children of Satan. I know it's not a popular statement, but it's absolutely scriptural (John 8:44). When we accept Jesus as our Lord and Savior, we are born again from a new birthplace and from a new Father!

23 having been born again, not of corruptible seed but incorruptible, through the word of God which lives and abides forever.

1 Peter 1:23 NKJV

4 You are of God, little children, and have overcome them, because He who is in you is greater than he who is in the world.

1 John 4:4 NKJV

Notice we were born of God. This three word phrase is short, but powerful. The word *of* means to indicate origin or source; this means that your origin is from God. There is no doubt about it – you are supernatural! Not only are you supernatural, but your heritage is phenomenal! If you are born again, there is no one more intelligent or powerful than your Heavenly Father.

Every cell of your body is permeated with the life and nature of God.

Too often we casually throw out the phrase that God is our Father without truly realizing what it all entails.

However, when you really start to meditate on the vastness of that statement, it starts to really play with your mind and stir up your spirit. God isn't just your Father, but He is your sustenance.

When God breathed into you, you became wall to wall Holy Spirit. Every cell of your body is permeated with the life and nature of God. There are personality traits about God that became yours as well just because of genetics! Just like a child takes on traits of their parents, we take on traits of our Father.

22 But the Holy Spirit produces this kind of fruit in our lives: love, joy, peace, patience, kindness, goodness, faithfulness, 23 gentleness, and self-control. There is no law against these things!

Galatians 5:22-23 NLT

The word *fruit* in Galatians 2:22 is the Greek word *karpos* which describes the fruit of one's body, such as a person's children or offspring.[3] When you were born again, these fruits began to produce God inside of you. The love of God, joy of God, faith of God, etc., began to work in your life! Why? Because you are like your dad!

Jesus Saved You From Your Excuses

When you were born again, you lost your excuses. You don't have a love problem anymore. You don't have a faith problem anymore. You don't have a joy problem anymore. Romans 5:5 says the love of God has been poured out in our spirit and we know that God never gives a little bit. God is an over the top, more than enough, net breaking, twelve baskets left over, too much giver! We can live on this earth like Jesus because we share the same DNA!

I get tired of hearing Christians say they can't change certain behaviors, lifestyles or attitudes because they were born that way. You may have been born that way from your momma, but when you were born again, all of your past went out the window. When you said, "Jesus be my Lord and Savior," He saved you from your past and saved you from your excuses.

Because of your Father, you have supernatural in your DNA.

When you were born again, God became your Father and now His very life and nature has flooded your spirit enabling you to believe, love, forgive and live like He would on the earth. It is simply a natural expression, a natural way of living because it is now your very nature.

When my son Jake was born, in the first moments of seeing him, Lacy and I both saw various aspects about Jake that was in us. Jake didn't have to work for it or try to get it; he simply had these common characteristics because he was our son. Over the next few months and years as his personality began to develop, there were things he would say and do as well as expressions he would make that was just like us – even in the way he slept! Why? It was in him; Jake has the DNA of his parents!

You aren't just a natural being; you are a supernatural being! Because of your Father, you have supernatural in your DNA!

Chapter 2
You Are A Spirit Being

I want to further explore the aspect of being a spirit. The Bible says in John 4:24 that God is a spirit. Well, if God is a spirit and He is our Father, wouldn't that make us spirit beings as well? Certainly! This is why we are told in the Scripture that God is the Father of spirits.

9 Furthermore, we have had human fathers who corrected us, and we paid them respect. Shall we not much more readily be in subjection to the Father of spirits and live?

Hebrews 12:9 NKJV

When we are born again, our spirit was born again, but nothing happened to our soul and body. This is why we are given instructions on what to do with our soul and body.

12 Don't copy the behavior and customs of this world, but let God transform you into a new person by changing the way you think. Then you will learn to know God's will for you, which is good and pleasing and perfect.

Romans 12:2 NLT

Notice we are to do something with our mind (our soul). We are to change the way we think so we can experience the results of what happened to our spirit. In the same way we are instructed to do something with our soul, we are also instructed to do something with our body.

What you see in the mirror each day is not you – it's your body; it's the house we live in. Look at what the Apostle Paul said about the body.

27 I discipline my body like an athlete, training it to do what it should…

1 Corinthians 9:27 NLT

The reason we have to discipline our body is because nothing happened to our body when we were born again. We will get a new body, but that will not happen until after we are gone from the earth (2 Corinthians 5:3).

The real you is a spirit. We are a spirit, we have a soul and we live in a body. It is through our spirit that we interact with the spiritual realm, with our soul that we interact with the intellectual and emotional realm and with our body that we interact with the physical realm.

This is a very basic foundational truth we must understand! This is one of the major truths Jesus was trying to help Nicodemus understand.

5 Jesus answered, "Most assuredly, I say to you, unless one is born of water and the Spirit, he cannot enter the kingdom of God. 6 That which is born of the flesh is flesh, and that which is born of the Spirit is spirit.

John 3:5-6 NKJV

Jesus said that if you are born of the Spirit – YOU ARE A SPIRIT! Nicodemus responded by asking Jesus how that was possible. Notice Jesus response to Nicodemus.

10 Jesus answered and said to him, "Are you the teacher of Israel, and do not know these things?

John 3:10 NKJV

Jesus expected Nicodemus to understand this basic truth since he was a leader in the religious community. Unfortunately, like Nicodemus, so many Christian leaders don't truly have a grasp on this truth. It's why we make statements like, "We're going soul winning today" or "Look how many souls we won for the kingdom today." We're not actually winning souls to Jesus; we are winning spirits to Jesus.

The supernatural should be natural because our nature is spirit.

We are more soul conscious and body conscious than we are spirit conscious. We go to school and educate our souls; we go to the gym and work on our bodies, but we rarely acknowledge the spiritual side of things, the aspect that makes us truly who we are: a spirit.

Jesus expected Nicodemus to already know this truth. Jesus went on to say, "If you don't understand this, how are you going to understand deeper things?" In other words, Jesus was letting him know this was a foundational truth; you must know you are a spirit being.

Now I want to present a thought for you to consider: as a spirit being, shouldn't the things of the spirit be more natural to interact with than the natural world? The answer is yes, but because of the way we are raised in this world, the things of the natural world are more real and normal than the things of the spirit world. After all, if you are born from a spiritual place, your Father is a spirit, and you are a spirit, shouldn't the spirit realm be more real to you than the natural realm?

The New Normal

Think about how most Christians talk in regards to hearing from God, moving in the supernatural, and experiencing the power of God. People act like it's abnormal for these things to happen and the reason they do is primarily because they don't have an understanding that we are spirit beings.

Because we are spirit beings, spiritual things should be natural to us, but we have allowed the natural world to become what is normal for us. Then, when we accidentally experience something miraculous, we act like it's abnormal. No, the supernatural should be natural for us because our nature is spirit.

18 While we do not look at the things which are seen, but at the things which are not seen. For the things which are seen are temporary, but the things which are not seen are eternal.

2 Corinthians 4:18 NKJV

Way, way too many Christians are looking at the seen things to determine whether the supernatural is working. We are looking to the things of the world to tell us if God has spoken, what God is doing, if His Word is true and who God made us to be. Friend, let me tell you something: *God didn't put us in this world to get our knowledge from the world. God put us in the world to change the world, not learn from it!* He put us in this world to change this world with the supernatural power of God, but most of us have no clue that we are a spirit being and most of those who do barely have a clue of what it actually means for us.

It is the unseen things that are eternal. It is the things of the spirit, the world we are from, that does not change and yet will change this world we currently live in. This is why we are told in 2 Corinthians 5:7 "We are to walk by faith and not by sight." Without adding or taking away from the

Scripture, you could also say, "We are to walk by the spirit and not by the flesh." It takes faith to walk by what you can't see, but it's what you can't see that will produce the results in the realm of what you can see.

When we begin to realize we are a spirit being united with God, it will totally revolutionize our lives; it will cause us to start looking to our spirit instead of our body. *We will start looking to the God on the inside of us instead of the god on the outside of us.*

Chapter 3
Hooked On A Feeling

One of the top reasons we are not seeing the supernatural like we should is because even though we know the faith lingo and we know the faith Scriptures, we aren't really walking by faith. Instead, we are walking by feelings, formulas and our flesh and calling it faith.

Faith always gets results and if you aren't getting results, then you have to humbly answer the question, "Is this really faith?" If we truly were walking by faith, we wouldn't be going through all the shenanigans we do to try and get the supernatural to happen.

I've been in church service after church service where you can tell the preacher is trying to work something up "so the power will show up." I've been in places where the preacher believed if you didn't wear a prayer shawl, the Holy Spirit wouldn't move in power. In other places, people think you have to blow a ram's horn before each service so that God will move. Some pastors can't preach or pray without a Hammond B3 screaming in the background. There are even some people who think God can't do anything unless you are wearing a three piece suit!

Now granted, there is nothing necessarily wrong with having these things, but when you depend on natural things to get you to be supernatural –something is wrong. I understand sometimes we can use a natural boost, but we should get to the point where we don't need a natural boost. The problem is, if you depend on something natural to get you into the supernatural, what happens when you don't have that natural thing? What happens if you are at the grocery store, someone needs a miracle and you don't have your prayer shawl, horn, hankie and 200 member choir?

And don't get me started on "protecting the anointing!" Some preacher's think they have to fly first class to protect it and others must have their filtered water at 72 degrees in order to protect the anointing. I could go on and on and on with this type of stuff! The problem is none of this has anything to do with your spirit man, but everything to do with your flesh. That tells me we are looking to our flesh to tell us whether anything spiritual can happen!

I want to look at a particular instance with Jesus and the Samaritan woman at the well.

1 Jesus knew the Pharisees had heard that he was baptizing and making more disciples than John 2 (though Jesus himself didn't baptize them—his disciples did). 3 So he left Judea and returned to Galilee. 4 He had to go through Samaria on the way. 5 Eventually he came to the Samaritan village of Sychar, near the field that Jacob gave to his son Joseph. 6 Jacob's well was there; and Jesus, tired from the long walk, sat wearily beside the well about noontime. 7 Soon a Samaritan woman came to draw water, and Jesus said to her, "Please give me a drink." 8 He was alone at the time because his disciples had gone into the village to buy some food. 9 The woman was surprised, for Jews refuse to have anything to do with Samaritans. She said to Jesus, "You are a Jew, and I am a Samaritan woman. Why are you asking me for a drink?" 10 Jesus replied, "If you only knew the gift God has for you and who you are speaking to, you would ask me, and

I would give you living water." 11 "But sir, you don't have a rope or a bucket," she said, "and this well is very deep. Where would you get this living water? 12 And besides, do you think you're greater than our ancestor Jacob, who gave us this well? How can you offer better water than he and his sons and his animals enjoyed?" 13 Jesus replied, "Anyone who drinks this water will soon become thirsty again. 14 But those who drink the water I give will never be thirsty again. It becomes a fresh, bubbling spring within them, giving them eternal life." 15 "Please, sir," the woman said, "give me this water! Then I'll never be thirsty again, and I won't have to come here to get water." 16 "Go and get your husband," Jesus told her. 17 "I don't have a husband," the woman replied. Jesus said, "You're right! You don't have a husband— 18 for you have had five husbands, and you aren't even married to the man you're living with now. You certainly spoke the truth!"

John 4:1-18 NLT

There are three main things I want you to see in this story. Number one, Jesus was tired and weary from his trip. Number two, His intent wasn't ministry; it was to sit down and get some water. Number three, even in the midst of all of this, He was still spiritual enough for the gifts of the Spirit to flow! Jesus was tired, thirsty and may have not felt like dealing with people, but He was still able to flow in the supernatural.

Now compare that to what goes on today. I understand that being tired certainly endeavors to amplify the voice of your flesh, but Jesus proved that despite how you feel, the supernatural will still flow in your life if you will look to the spirit instead of the flesh.

16 But I say, walk and live [habitually] in the [Holy] Spirit [responsive to and controlled and guided by the Spirit]; then you will certainly not gratify the cravings and desires of the flesh (of human nature without God).

Galatians 5:16 AMP

We are looking to the flesh to tell us if we can be spiritual; instead, we should be looking to the spirit to show us how we should act in the natural. This is why most of Christianity is sitting around wondering why the supernatural is not being experienced on a normal basis.

Too many Christians are hooked on a feeling. Listen to how many of your Christian friends and church folk mention their feelings! You will hear statements like this all the time:

- •"I just don't feel like I have enough faith."
- •"I don't feel like God loves me."
- •"I don't feel like I can forgive them."
- •"I don't feel like I am anointed enough to pray for the sick."

You will notice that when people start talking about their feelings, it is almost always as a disqualifier as to why they can't do what God said they can do!

3 Are you so foolish? Having begun in the Spirit, are you now being made perfect by the flesh?
Galatians 3:3 NKJV

The Apostle Paul had this question for the church of Galatia and it's the question we should be asking modern day faith people. When we were born again, we started out in the spirit; however, because of growing up and becoming accustomed to the world's way of doing life, we allowed ourselves to become carnally minded instead of spiritually minded. Your flesh, your emotions and your feelings will always tell you that you can't do what the Word says you can do.

No Condemnation

1 There is therefore now no condemnation to those who are in Christ Jesus, who do not walk according to the flesh, but according to the Spirit. 5 For those who live according to the flesh set their minds on the things of the flesh, but those who live according to the Spirit, the things of the Spirit. 6 For to be carnally minded is death, but to be spiritually minded is life and peace.

Romans 8:1, 5-6 NKJV

Feelings are the voice of our flesh and when you walk according to your feelings, you will almost always feel condemned. Your feelings will scream that you are lacking in faith, that you didn't read enough of your Bible today or that you just aren't righteous enough for God to work through you. Feelings will almost always side with religion!

It's not about how you feel, but what you know.

God tells us when we begin to think about how we feel, we will live that way; conversely, when we begin to think about the realities of who we are in the spirit, the result will be life and peace. Remember, it's not about what you feel, but what you know! If we will walk according to the realities of our union with Christ, our feelings will not be able to stop the supernatural from flowing in our life.

There was another man we are told about in the Bible that is world renowned. Christian and non-Christian alike have heard of him; his name was Samson. Samson lived around 1200-1000 B.C. and was a man powerfully used by God to deliver the Israelites from the Philistines. By the Holy Spirit, Samson was able to perform feats of strength only to be matched by Superman himself!

5 As Samson and his parents were going down to Timnah, a young lion suddenly attacked Samson near the vineyards of Timnah. 6 At that moment the Spirit of the Lord came powerfully upon him, and he ripped the lion's jaws apart with his bare hands. He did it as easily as if it were a young goat. But he didn't tell his father or mother about it.

Judges 14:4-6 NLT

We see here that the Holy Spirit came upon Samson in a mighty way empowering him to kill the lion. Now this is important because so many of us have the idea that in order for the supernatural power of God to flow through us, we need to feel something. In this instance, we just assume that Samson felt something to make him feel strong and therefore he went after the lion. Here is another instance of the Holy Spirit empowering Samson to do the impossible.

11 So 3,000 men of Judah went down to get Samson at the cave in the rock of Etam. They said to Samson, "Don't you realize the Philistines rule over us? What are you doing to us?" But Samson replied, "I only did to them what they did to me." 12 But the men of Judah told him, "We have come to tie you up and hand you over to the Philistines." "All right," Samson said. "But promise that you won't kill me yourselves." 13 "We will only tie you up and hand you over to the Philistines," they replied. "We won't kill you." So they tied him up with two new ropes and brought him up from the rock. 14 As Samson arrived at Lehi, the Philistines came shouting in triumph. But the Spirit of the Lord came powerfully upon Samson, and he snapped the ropes on his arms as if they were burnt strands of flax, and they fell from his wrists. 15 Then he found the jawbone of a recently killed donkey. He picked it up and killed 1,000 Philistines with it.

Judges 15:11-15 NLT

Again, we see the Holy Spirit come upon Samson mightily causing him to operate in supernatural strength. This time, he broke through two new ropes and killed one thousand Philistines with a jawbone. Many people assume Samson had some feeling come upon him and because of that feeling, he knew he could take on an enemy of one thousand men. I mean, wouldn't it take some type of supernatural sign for you to think you could defeat one thousand men all by yourself?

As a side note, notice that Samson used a jawbone of a recently killed donkey. It was a sin for an Israelite to touch dead things; so, according to the law, Samson sinned. Not only did he operate in the supernatural, but he obviously didn't think grabbing the jawbone would keep him from operating in the supernatural. This is important and we will look at the issue of sin and condemnation later, but it's interesting that even in his sin, Samson still moved in the power of the Holy Spirit. Sin is never okay, but it's worth noting condemnation didn't stop Samson from thinking he could do the impossible.

So we see two instances of the Holy Spirit coming upon Samson and as a result, Samson operated in the supernatural. In Judges 16, we see Samson's winning streak come to an end. Delilah starts really putting the pressure on Samson as to the source of his strength and unfortunately, Samson allowed the lust of a woman to win out over his loyalty towards God.

15 Then Delilah pouted, "How can you tell me, 'I love you,' when you don't share your secrets with me? You've made fun of me three times now, and you still haven't told me what makes you so strong!" 16 She tormented him with her nagging day after day until he was sick to death of it. 17 Finally, Samson shared his secret with her. "My hair has never been cut," he confessed, "for I was dedicated to God as a Nazirite from birth. If my head were shaved, my strength would leave me, and I would become as weak as anyone else." 18 Delilah realized he had finally told her the truth, so she sent for the Philistine rulers. "Come back one more time," she said, "for he has finally told me his secret." So the Philistine rulers returned with the money in their hands. 19 Delilah lulled Samson to sleep with his head in her lap, and then she called in a man to shave off the seven locks of his hair. In this way she began to bring him down, and his strength left him. 20 Then she cried out, "Samson! The Philistines have come to capture you!" When he woke up, he thought, "I will do

**as before and shake myself free." But he didn't realize
the Lord had left him.**

Judges 16:15-20 NLT

In this passage of Scripture, we are given some really good nuggets of information. First, Samson awoke and said to himself, "I'll get up and do what I've always done." Secondly, Samson did not know the Holy Spirit had left. (As a side note, remember as a Christian under the New Covenant, the Holy Spirit never leaves us; He resides within us. Under the Old Covenant, the Holy Spirit did not reside within the people; He only came upon people to equip them for a job.)

So because Samson didn't know the Holy Spirit had left him and he still got up to go after the Philistines, this tells us something extremely important: Samson didn't have some special feeling to let him know supernatural strength was available. This is vitally important for you and me! All the times Samson was operating in the supernatural, it wasn't because of a feeling, but because of faith in what he knew.

**32 How much more do I need to say? It would take
too long to recount the stories of the faith of Gideon,**

Barak, Samson, Jephthah, David, Samuel, and all the prophets. 33 By faith these people overthrew kingdoms, ruled with justice, and received what God had promised them. They shut the mouths of lions, 34 quenched the flames of fire, and escaped death by the edge of the sword. Their weakness was turned to strength. They became strong in battle and put whole armies to flight.

Hebrews 11:32-34 NLT

Walking in the supernatural has nothing to do with how you feel, but everything to do with what you know! This is why faith is necessary and why we are to walk by faith and not by sight!

Now I am not saying there aren't times when our flesh might feel something. Even with Jesus, we know there were times when he felt the power of God flow through Him. A great example is found in Mark 5.

27 She had heard about Jesus, so she came up behind him through the crowd and touched his robe. 28 For she thought to herself, "If I can just touch his robe, I will be healed." 29 Immediately the bleeding stopped, and she could feel in her body that she had been

healed of her terrible condition. 30 Jesus realized at once that healing power had gone out from him, so he turned around in the crowd and asked, "Who touched my robe?"

Mark 5:27-30 NLT

In this instance we see Jesus felt something, but it didn't cause Him to step out in faith; His feeling something was the result of the woman taking her healing. In most of the other instances of Jesus healing people, as well as casting out devils, calming storms, multiplying food, etc, we are not given even a hint that Jesus felt something; instead, we see Him being led by the Holy Spirit and acting on what He knew by the Holy Spirit.

I Don't Feel Spiritual

I hear Christians all the time make the comment "I just don't feel spiritual." Have you ever thought about that statement? When you really take a step back and think about it, it makes no sense at all. How can you possibly feel spiritual? You can't! Feelings are the voice of your flesh; things of the spirit have nothing to do with the things of the flesh. It is impossible for your feelings to truly communicate anything of the spirit.

Do you realize the absurdity as to how the word *feelings* is used? We use it to describe our relationships, our job, our emotional state, the physical state of our body, our stress level, etc. and the list goes on and on to include what Jesus died and paid for with His blood.

We use the word *feelings* so freely and flippantly that we've allowed it to carry over to spiritual things and it is one of the top reasons most Christians live defeated lives. Please understand this: you will never feel spiritual enough to get the job done because your feelings are associated with your unsaved soul and flesh. Satan will always endeavor to use these things to get you to disqualify yourself.

Feelings Are Fickle

In addition, your feelings are fickle; they are always changing. How many times do you feel happy or sad during the day? How many times do you feel stressed and relaxed during the day? It is because your feelings are the voice of your flesh and your flesh is always subject to change.

While we do not look at the things which are seen, but the things which are unseen. For the things that are seen are temporary, but the things which are unseen are eternal.

2 Corinthians 4:18

If you are looking to feelings to tell you when you are spiritual, your "spirituality" is going to constantly fluctuate. Your feelings are like the weather. In Texas, if you don't like the weather, wait a few hours and it will change. Growing up in Texas, I would go to school and bring a change of clothes because it would usually be cool enough for a sweater in the mornings and hot enough for a T-shirt and shorts in the afternoon. After living in Arkansas for some time, I found out the weather is even crazier! I'll never forget this one week in March 2014. We had nice warm weather for about two weeks and then out of nowhere, we got about 6 inches of snow!

As crazy as the weather is, your feelings are even worse. Your feelings can fluctuate by the second! The big problem is the people who need Jesus can't have your spirituality fluctuating like the weather.

We often forget the importance of this – people are

depending on you; your family, friends and people you haven't met yet are depending on you to know you are spiritual and to manifest the supernatural. When problems arise, if you are depending on your feelings to tell you if you are spiritual at the moment, your feelings WILL ALWAYS tell you the same answer: "Right now, you are not spiritual enough!"

What if Jesus would have discerned his spirituality by his feelings? There is no way He would have operated in the supernatural that day with the woman at the well. Instead, Jesus was naturally supernatural. Jesus wasn't led by His feelings, but led by His righteousness. He knew Who He was and Who was operating within Him and that is called faith.

Faith Versus Feelings

Remember, we are to walk by faith and not by sight; walk by spirit and not by flesh. Faith is based on knowledge of God's Word. Romans 10:17 says that faith comes by hearing the Word of God. Notice faith is based on God's Word, not your feelings. When you know what you have and who you are through your union with Christ, what you know will supersede how you feel. This is why according to 2 Corinthians 4:18, we are to look to the things that are eternal, steadfast and unchanging. When you do this, your sense of spirituality won't be changing like the weather! When your sense of spirituality is constant, then your ability to flow in the supernatural will be constant and that is when life starts to get really fun!

Chapter 4
Take Inventory
Of The Spirit

When I was in college, I worked for a retail business. At certain times of the year, we were required to take inventory of what was in the showroom as well as the storage warehouse. The reason we took inventory was so we knew exactly what products and the quantity of those products we had in stock.

Did you know we do the same thing individually every day? You may not be taking inventory at your job, but you take inventory of your spirit, soul and body all of the time. When you wake up in the mornings, you take inventory of your body. You check and see whether you are rested or tired, you check your face, teeth, hair and skin; essentially, when you want to take inventory of your body, you don't check your spirit or soul do you? No, you look at your body. That would be like a machine shop taking inventory at the warehouse owned by a clothing store! The clothing store can't give proper information to the machine shop.

In the same manner, we take inventory of our soul quite often too. We are very aware of our feelings and are constantly checking our feelings. We find out we are mad, glad, happy, sad, depressed, anxious, fearful, worried and so forth. When we do inventory on our soul, do we go to the body's warehouse? No, because our body can't tell us anything about our soul. You could say that the warehouse of your soul contains your emotions and feelings and the warehouse for your body contains all the information that comes from what you can see, hear, smell, taste and touch.

Much like our body and soul, every so often we take inventory of our spirit. Unfortunately, we don't take inventory of our spirit very well at all. Do you know why? The vast majority of Christians go to the wrong warehouse! Rarely do we check our spirit's warehouse to take inventory; usually, we go to the soul's warehouse to tell us what we have and how we are doing spiritually. This is why you hear Christians make statements like: "I don't feel righteous." "I don't feel forgiven." "I don't feel like God loves me." "I don't feel like I have enough faith." The list goes on and on.

Because we check the wrong warehouse, we often get a flawed inventory of ourselves spiritually which always results in us short changing ourselves and eventually failing miserably.

63 The Spirit alone gives eternal life. Human effort accomplished nothing. And the very words I have spoken to you are spirit and life.

John 6:63 NLT

When you take inventory of your spirit, you need to go to the Word of God. Jesus said His words are spirit. So if you want to know what you are like spiritually and what you have spiritually, you need to look at what Jesus had to say. After all, you are one with Him and unified with Him; what is flowing through Him is flowing through you. If I want to take inventory of myself spiritually, I would be a fool to check my emotions. I will never succeed spiritually if I am always checking my emotions and feelings to see if I can do what God told me to do.

The Deaf Woman At Walmart

Several years ago, I was sitting in the Walmart parking lot in Bryan, Texas. I had dropped Lacy off so she could get some groceries and I decided to just stay in the car and read my Bible until she was done. A few minutes later, a woman knocked on my window. I rolled my window down and she showed me a pen and pad of paper she was selling for two dollars. She wrote on the pad of paper that she was deaf and did this as a means to support herself. Well, I told her I didn't have any cash on me and so she left – and I went back to reading my Bible. A few seconds later, I realized what I did. Here I was, a faith-filled spirit-filled preacher with a great emphasis of healing in our ministry and I just told a deaf lady to leave me alone because I was reading my Bible!

Well, I told the Lord I was sorry and waited for Lacy to finish shopping. When Lacy was done, I picked her up and I began driving through the parking lot looking for the deaf lady. As soon as I spotted her, I got out of our vehicle and walked over to her. Through pencil and paper, I told her I didn't have any cash on me, but I had something better. I began talking to her about healing, but she stopped me and told me that over the years, plenty of people had prayed for her and nothing had happened. So, I readily saw that she wasn't really open to what I had to say at that moment. Then, I did something that came directly from my spirit. I wrote down on the pad of paper, "If you will come to church on Sunday, I'll bet you one hundred dollars you walk out healed." Well, that certainly got her attention; she immediately asked for the address of the church and service times. With tears in her eyes, she gave me a hug and signed that she would be there.

I got into our car and Lacy asked me what happened (she assumed she got healed since the woman was crying and hugging me.) I told Lacy I bet the deaf woman one hundred dollars that God would heal her on Sunday to which Lacy replied, "Are you crazy?" She then asked, "Can you do that?" I then asked myself the same question and my only response was, "Well, I guess we will find out!"

This encounter happened on a Monday which gave me all week to think about this crazy bet I made with the deaf woman at Walmart. Once I got over the initial shock of what I had actually done, I started spending some quality time that week praying in tongues and meditating on my union with Christ.

So, Sunday arrives. Now usually, I will go to church a few hours early just to spend some time alone and get my mind where it needs to be for the service. When I arrived to church, I got a text from our worship leader that they were sick and would not be able to make it to the morning service. At that season of our church, although we had a good band, we didn't have anyone to lead – so that left me. I can sing a little and play the keys, so I dropped what I was doing and started working on a worship set for that morning.

When the worship team arrived for practice, I was already a little flustered from being rushed and unprepared. Needless to say, practice didn't go very well which led to a mediocre worship service. As soon as we finished with worship, Lacy came up on the platform to welcome the people. While I was walking down the platform, our head usher put a note in my hand. When I looked at it, I literally shuddered in fear. The note read, "The deaf lady from Walmart is here."

All I could think of was that I did not feel very spiritual at that moment, much less ready to take on healing for a deaf woman. Then this thought came to me: "Just have the deaf woman come to your office after the service. If you pray for her and nothing happens, you can give her the one hundred dollars and no one will have to know about it." I literally thought that! No joke! But at that point in my life and ministry, I had learned enough to know that I would never get results like that.

You see, if you want to experience the supernatural, you just have to walk the plank and jump off with nothing but the Word of God under your feet. I had a choice to be spiritual or carnal, to be moved by my spirit or moved by my feelings. I knew God was still God despite the way that I felt, so I just stopped the service and began to tell the congregation about my encounter with the deaf woman.

As I was telling the story, I began to sense the power of God. I went from feeling like a rotten worm under a bucket of scum to feeling like Superman! I then told the deaf woman to stand up. I walked over to her and commanded her ears to open up in the Name of Jesus! I asked her what she could hear and she said she could actually hear a little bit. Well, that got me and the congregation excited because she couldn't hear anything before! So I put my hands on her ears again and commanded them to be healed in the Name of Jesus. I asked again, "What can you hear?" She said she could hear even better. I then told her to just sit down and enjoy the rest of the service and whenever her hearing was completely restored, to raise her hand to let us know.

God is my witness, about fifteen minutes went by and she raised up her hand. I asked her how she was doing and she told us she could her perfectly! Well, at that point, the congregation just went nuts; I think I may have even run a few laps around the auditorium! At the end of the service, even though God healed her, I gave her the one hundred dollar bill just to be a blessing to her. We then took a picture together in the foyer with her holding the one hundred dollar bill.

That woman's healing may have never happened without that bet. Obviously, that didn't come from my head; I spoke that directly from my spirit. It certainly wouldn't have happened had I decided to be a coward that Sunday morning and be feeling led instead of spirit led.

Romans 8:14 says, "For as many as are led by the Spirit of God, these are the sons of God." The literal Greek brings out that those who are led by the Spirit of God are the mature sons of God. It takes a mature person to put your feelings to the wayside and follow the Holy Spirit. When you do that, the supernatural becomes natural because you stop looking at yourself and you start looking at Him. You don't have to feel supernatural to experience the supernatural. Some of the greatest miracles I have ever experienced happened when I felt as dry as a bone.

Starting A Church From Scratch

I remember when the Lord told me it was time to go to Texas and start a church. At the time, I was twenty eight years old. In the natural sense, outside of my two years at Rhema Bible Training Center, that was all the ministry training I had. I had never been a youth pastor, children's pastor or even the church custodian, much less a senior pastor. I had never started a church from scratch before and didn't know anyone who had either. I had no mentor, no one to ask questions or get advice; looking at my knowledge and experience, this seemed like a bad idea – and that wasn't taking into account the financial piece of it! Lacy and I had no money. We had no partners and no church supporting us; we had no financial backing whatsoever. Take inventory of that! This looked like a disaster in the making! No knowledge, no experience, no money, no support – lots of no's!

I remember sitting on our upstairs porch around 11pm on a cool night in October of 2005 in Beaumont, Texas. I had been spending an extended amount of time praying for a few weeks and on that night, something just dropped within me; I knew it was time to move forward in preparation for the church. I was excited as I had been patiently waiting on God to give us the go for several years. However, over the next few weeks, I started checking the warehouse of my soul to get the status of things spiritually and oh how it didn't look good.

The reality of our lack of finances started screaming at me as well as the fact that naturally, I had no clue as to how to start a church from scratch. Sure, for years I had thought about names, marketing strategies, outreach activities and messages, but then I started wondering, "How are we going to get people to even show up?" "Can I really do this?"

That right there was my sign I was taking inventory in the wrong warehouse. I got a hold of myself and began dwelling on the fact that the Spirit of God who is my leader, guide and revealer of Truth was living on the inside of me. I began meditating on the truth that I was the righteousness of God in Christ and that I could do all things through Christ who strengthened me. I chewed on truths such as being complete in Christ, that I had the favor and blessing of God upon my life and many other spiritual realities. Soon, I was back where God wanted me to be – ready to conquer the world and fulfill His plan for my life.

As soon as I started looking in the right warehouse, I started getting excited again and brewing with confidence. I knew if we simply listened and obeyed the leading of the Holy Spirit, everything would turn out great. We ended up launching the church in September of 2006 in a 4,000 square foot restaurant in College Station, Texas that we leased for one year - God immediately began to bless us.

In December of 2007, we purchased a 16,000 square foot building worth 1.2 million dollars and we had over one hundred thousand dollars in the bank. Some people asked me how we did it, expecting me to give them some formula or "how to" program. Sure, we had some trials and I made plenty of mistakes, but the supernatural things happened so naturally because I was simply relying on Him.

In March of 2012, I knew it was time to leave Texas. At that time, we had been pastoring for almost 6 years and Lacy and I also had a very successful day care and preschool that we owned and operated. I had never wanted to leave

Texas. I thought we would be there until Jesus came back, but I knew it was time to go. Lacy had been sensing it for about a year, but I was too stubborn to listen. I had been sensing it too, but my emotions and feelings were telling my spirit to shut up! By March, I finally told my feelings to shut up and we started searching to find out where God was leading us to go. It took a few months, but in June 2012 we stepped down as the pastors of the church we planted and turned it over to another couple.

Feelings will talk you out of God's plan for your life.

The next month we moved to Jonesboro, Arkansas and took over a church that was established in the early 80's. By this time, we had some experience and boy did we need it. The church had peaked in the late 80's and had slowly been declining ever since. When we arrived, it was on its death bed and needed a miracle. There were so many issues in the church that I had people asking me if I had lost my mind by accepting the pastorate of this church!

It was not a situation for the faint of heart and thin skinned. It was like walking into a war zone, but we relied on God's grace and supernaturally, things began to fall in place.

God's wisdom and grace was evident as He supernaturally helped Lacy and I to make simple decisions that on the outside looked extremely hard. God did a miracle in the church and it went from survival mode to thriving mode within two years. It literally was the easiest thing I've ever done in ministry and easily one of the greatest miracles of divine intervention I've ever experienced.

I can honestly say the supernatural was naturally flowing through the whole process and it was because we had followed the Holy Spirit and kept checking the right warehouse for inventory. You'll find that there is a grace for your place. If you will learn to be led by the Holy Spirit, He will always make sure you are in the right place at the right time - that is His job. You job is to get to the right place and then keep taking inventory of who you are in Christ; when you do that, the grace of God will flow like a river!

If you don't learn to take spiritual inventory from the Word, your feelings, emotions, and circumstances will always talk you out of God's plan for your life. Your feelings are fickle and will always change. They are not reliable and if left unchecked, will side with religion and the devil.

If you want to experience the supernatural, this is extremely important. Look at your spiritual inventory often! One of my purposes in this book is to help you get a good look at your inventory so you will never doubt again who you are and what you possess. When you do, the supernatural will become as normal and natural in your life as breathing.

Chapter 5

Think On Heaven

Your actions are preceded by your thoughts, so if you are going to act supernatural, you must think supernatural. This is the reason we are given so many instructions in the New Testament about our thoughts.

2 Set your mind on things above, not on things on the earth.

Colossians 3:2 NKJV

What are we to put our mind on? We are to be thinking about the realities of Heaven, not the ever changing facts of the earth. We see this with Jesus. Jesus was constantly talking about the fact that He was from Heaven and was going back to Heaven. What you talk about is what you think about and what you think about is what you will do.

Don't ever forget that Jesus was doing life as a human being just like us. The Bible says in Hebrews 4:15 that Jesus dealt with the very same temptations as we do – one of those temptations being to allow the realities of this world to supersede the realities of Heaven.

Set Your Mind

5 For those who live according to the flesh set their minds on the things of the flesh, but those who live according to the Spirit, the things of the Spirit.

Romans 8:5 NKJV

Notice we are told to "set our minds." This tells us we not only have control over what we think, but we are also the one responsible for what we think on. Basically, you can't ask God to control your thoughts; you are the one who is to control your thoughts.

You are the one who chooses whether you are going to experience the supernatural or not. If you want to live a supernatural life, it means you must set your mind on the things of Heaven; you must set your mind on spiritual realities instead of natural facts. It's very similar to what we are told in 2 Corinthians 4.

18 While we do not look at the things which are seen, but the things which are unseen. For the things that are seen are temporary, but the things which are unseen are eternal.

2 Corinthians 4:18 NKJV

To live naturally supernatural requires a change in our perspective and a shift in our thinking.

8 And now, dear brothers and sisters, one final thing. Fix your thoughts on what is true, and honorable, and right, and pure, and lovely, and admirable. Think about things that are excellent and worthy of praise.

Philippians 4:8 NLT

What are we to think on? We are to think on what is true and of a good report. The reports from the world always change, but God's report never changes. The report of the Lord is that we always win! The report of the world is that sometimes you win, sometimes you lose – you just never know what is going to happen. *However, if you are going to change what is always changing, then your mind needs to be on what doesn't change.*

Think about the realities of Heaven. There is no sickness, lack, condemnation, fear, or weakness. The things of Heaven supersede the things of this earth. God's will is that earth operates with the efficiency and blessing of Heaven! Heaven is where you are from! Heaven is your birthplace and citizenship. You are simply here on the earth sent by God to do a job and then go home; yet, while you are here, you are operating according to the laws of Heaven and the economy of Heaven!

The major reason God wants your mind on the things of Heaven is because that is where you are from!

18 For many walk, of whom I have told you often, and now tell you even weeping, that they are the enemies of the cross of Christ: 19 whose end is destruction, whose god is their belly, and whose glory is in their shame—who set their mind on earthly things. 20 For our citizenship is in heaven, from which we also eagerly wait for the Savior, the Lord Jesus Christ.

Philippians 3:18-20 NKJV

When you set your mind on earthly things, when you set your mind on this world's system, you will walk according to it because that is what will be real to you. Paul tells us that our citizenship is in Heaven; so that is where we are to set our mind on – Heaven. Heaven is where we were born from; we are citizens of Heaven by birth! We are to think on Heaven, think about the realities of Heaven, and live from Heaven so we can manifest Heaven on earth.

Change The Way You Think

If you want to walk in the supernatural and it be natural for you, then your thoughts and meditations will have to be on the supernatural. You aren't going to act on something that isn't real to you; this is why we are told to change the way we think.

2 Don't copy the behavior and customs of this world, but let God transform you into a new person by changing the way you think. Then you will learn to know God's will for you, which is good and pleasing and perfect.

Romans 12:2 NLT

We have to renew our mind to God's reality and that will only happen by continually keeping our mind on the truths of God. If you are going to live naturally supernatural, then when the circumstances of life suddenly hit, you need the truths of God's Word to come flooding out. You need the realities of Heaven to be so real to you that they are a normal part of your natural, everyday existence – but this will only happen by continually thinking about them.

7 For as he thinks in his heart, so is he.

Proverbs 23:7 NKJV

This is why it's so important to know you are a spirit being. When you begin to think like this, you'll stop looking so much to your feelings. Your feelings will not be able to override who you know yourself to be. You are a spirit, a supernatural being, with a supernatural Father, born from a supernatural place!

Chapter 6
Living In Him

17 This means that anyone who belongs to Christ has become a new person. The old life is gone; a new life has begun!

2 Corinthians 5:17 NLT

When we accepted Jesus as our Lord and Savior, something phenomenal happened to you: your spirit, the real you, became brand new and you were unified with Christ. Your union with Christ blew the door open to the supernatural. Before Jesus, the devil was your daddy; after Jesus, God is your daddy.

We've already seen briefly that salvation gave you a new Father, a new home and a new birth, but over these next few chapters, I want to reveal to you key aspects of what Jesus did for you that enables you to live a naturally supernatural life. Everything that we are going to look at from this point on has its foundation in your union with Christ. It is because of Him and through Him that all of these things are possible.

20 I have been crucified with Christ; it is no longer I who live, but Christ lives in me; and the life which I now live in the flesh I live by faith in the Son of God, who loved me and gave Himself for me. 21 I do not set aside the grace of God...

Galatians 2:20-21 NKJV

The life we live is to be a life in Christ. Notice in the above text that it's "Christ who lives in me." The Distilled Translation states, "..it is simply Jesus using my body." It's much more than just living life and trusting in Jesus. I'm living this life IN HIM. I stopped doing life in and of myself because it's no longer just me living. I am living life united with Christ, so now I am doing life through Jesus. The life I live in the flesh, I live by faith in Him!

Once I stop doing life out of my union with Christ, I start getting into works and I set aside the grace of God. The deal is this: you can't operate in the grace of God outside of your union with Christ; yet, this is why so many good hearted, spirit-filled Christians today are trying to experience the supernatural to no avail.

> **28 For in Him we live and move and have our being, as also some of your own poets have said, 'For we are also His offspring.'**
>
> **Acts 17:28 NKJV**

This has absolutely been one of my cornerstone scriptures. I live, move and have my being in Him. I view myself as living this life through Him. When I have my being in Him, how could I possibly fail? How could I possibly not have enough? How could I not get the same results as Jesus when I am living life through Him?

The Same Anointing

So now when I minister healing to people, I view my hands as Jesus hands touching them and I tell them, "It is no different me touching you than Jesus touching you because His life is flowing through my hands." I view Jesus anointing to heal the sick, raise the dead and cast out devils as the same anointing in me; after all, how could I not have that same anointing when Christ lives in me.

> **27 For God wanted them to know that the riches and glory of Christ are for you Gentiles, too. And this is the secret: Christ lives in you. This gives you assurance of sharing his glory.**
>
> **Colossians 1:27 NLT**

The word *Christ* is the Greek word *Christos* which means the Anointed One and His anointing. So we need to read the Scripture like this: "The Anointed One and His Anointing lives in you. This gives you the assurance of sharing His glory." What a powerful truth! This should begin to change your perspective when you pray for and minister to people. You don't need to try and get anointed; you are anointed with Christ's anointing!

Doing The Works

The life we are to live is no different than the life Jesus lived on the earth. Jesus didn't do life by Himself; He did life in union with the Father.

> **10 Do you not believe that I am in the Father, and the Father in Me? The words that I speak to you I do not**

speak on My own authority; but the Father who dwells in Me does the works.

John 14:10 NKJV

Notice Jesus didn't take credit for the miracles; Jesus stated it was the Father who dwelled in Him that was doing the works. This relationship Jesus had with the Father is the same relationship we have with Jesus. We aren't doing the miraculous in and of ourselves; it happens through Christ who lives within us. It is Christ doing the works!

After telling us how the works were done, Jesus makes a powerful statement about our ability to flow in the power of God.

12 Most assuredly, I say to you, he who believes in Me, the works that I do he will do also; and greater works than these he will do, because I go to My Father.

John 14:12 NKJV

Why would we be able to do the works? The result of Jesus going to the Father was that He was going to send the Holy Spirit to us; the same Spirit that worked in Jesus was now going to work in us!

16 And I will pray the Father, and He will give you another Helper, that He may abide with you forever— 17 the Spirit of truth, whom the world cannot receive, because it neither sees Him nor knows Him; but you know Him, for He dwells with you and will be in you.

John 14:16-17 NKJV

Get Rid Of The Gimmicks

Many of us are working so hard to get the supernatural to happen that we are looking to gimmicks and natural formulas to experience the supernatural. If we would simply begin to look at who we are in Christ and our union with Christ, the supernatural would become a natural occurrence in our lives.

Instead of trying to do, we need to simply be. We're trying to do it on our own. That's why when you see people relying on natural things to get the supernatural to happen, it's a glaring sign they have stepped away from their union with Christ and are trying to make it happen on their own.

I'll never forget when we moved to Jonesboro to begin pastoring Trinity Church. A few weeks before we arrived, there was a guest minister who said he was going to anoint the pulpit with oil so I would be even more anointed. When I was told of this, even though I appreciated the gesture, I couldn't help but laugh. The concept was that by putting oil on the pulpit and laying a prayer shawl across it, that was going to help me be more anointed.

Do you see any lunacy in that? I'm sorry, but no natural act by a man is going to help me be more anointed; although, it sounds real spiritual doesn't it? I've got the Spirit of Christ living within me; what is your olive oil and shawl on a pulpit going to add to the Christ?

Jesus And His Union With God

We must understand our union with Christ and how to operate in it. The best way to do that is to look at Jesus and how He operated in His union with the Father.

19 Then Jesus answered and said to them, "Most assuredly, I say to you, the Son can do nothing of Himself, but what He sees the Father do; for whatever He does, the Son also does in like manner.

John 5:19 NKJV

Again, notice what Jesus said. Even though He was the

Son of God, Jesus couldn't do what He did all by Himself. One essential truth we must understand about Jesus was that even though He is the Son of God, He did life on the earth as a man.

> **6 Who, although being essentially one with God and in the form of God possessing the fullness of the attributes which make God God], did not think this equality with God was a thing to be eagerly grasped or retained, 7 But stripped Himself [of all privileges and rightful dignity], so as to assume the guise of a servant (slave), in that He became like men and was born a human being.**
>
> **Philippians 2:6-7 AMP**

Jesus essentially laid aside everything that gave Himself an advantage in life so He could do life as a human being. He experienced the same temptations we experience. Jesus had to deal with thoughts of fear, doubt and unbelief as well as dealing with His emotions and feelings just like us; this is why He was able to be our High Priest.

It's interesting that Jesus referred to Himself as the Son of Man more than He did as the Son of God. Now please understand, I am not taking away from the deity of Jesus;

however, if we are going to do the works of Jesus and experience the supernatural like Jesus, we must understand He did life just like you and I. Jesus lived life as a human divinely connected to God.

38 And you know that God anointed Jesus of Nazareth with the Holy Spirit and with power. Then Jesus went around doing good and healing all who were oppressed by the devil, for God was with him.

Acts 10:38 NLT

This is also the reason that Jesus had to be anointed. God doesn't need to be anointed, but a man does and that is why God anointed Jesus with the Holy Spirit so that the supernatural could flow through Him. This is the same reason Jesus had to send the Holy Spirit to you and I.

We needed to be anointed and have the supernatural flow through us; although, for the supernatural to be natural, these spiritual realities must become natural and normal realties to us. This is why it's so important to look at the life of Jesus and see how He operated in the supernatural, how He did things and why He did things. The foundation for it all was His union with God.

Jesus constantly talked of His union with God. Not only

did He understand that it was the Father on the inside of Him doing the works, He also knew God was always with Him.

28 Then Jesus said to them, "When you lift up the Son of Man, then you will know that I am He, and that I do nothing of Myself; but as My Father taught Me, I speak these things. 29 And He who sent Me is with Me. The Father has not left Me alone, for I always do those things that please Him."

John 8:28-29 NKJV

God Is Always With Us

You'll never find Jesus praying for God to show up, yet how many times do we hear it in our church services? Jesus didn't need to pray for God to show up, because number one, God is omnipresent and number two, God was living with Him.

Think about how many times you hear preachers praying from the pulpit for God to show up. After we pray for Him to show up, it usually leads to either hoping and waiting for God to do something so we know He is there or for those who are really eager, to start going through fleshy actions to make something happen. In all reality, if you know God is already there and you know God is with you, you don't need to wait for God; all you need to do is move.

If you want to see God move, then move! If you are the body of Christ, start moving and when you move, God moves. Jesus wasn't sitting back waiting on a move of God; Jesus realized He was a move of God and we need to realize we are a move of God waiting to happen! I'm convinced the reason we aren't seeing more moves of God is because instead of moving, most Christians are sitting, twiddling their thumbs and waiting on God to do something.

Chapter 7
Effortless Results

5 "Yes, I am the vine; you are the branches. Those who remain in me, and I in them, will produce much fruit. For apart from me you can do nothing.

John 15:5 NLT

Have you ever looked at a fruit tree and seen the branch struggle to produce fruit? You've never seen the struggle because it doesn't have to struggle; the role of the branch is to just stay connected and receive of the life that is flowing into it from the trunk. It is the trunk and roots that do all the work!

This is why Jesus told us in John 15:5 that He is the vine and we are the branches. He went on to say that when the branch is connected to the vine, fruit is the automatic result. While the trunk and roots do the work, all the branch has to do is just be connected and it will naturally produce fruit! Do you get it? This is called grace my friend. You and I were not called to struggle to get the supernatural to happen; we were called to rest – only when that happens will the supernatural naturally happen in your life.

Be Instead Of Do

If you are trying to make something happen, that is your sign that you have become disconnected; you've stopped being aware that you are connected and united to Jesus! As human beings, it is in our nature to do and make things happen. When we need money, the first natural thought is "What can I do?" We then begin thinking about second jobs, loans, business ideas, etc., instead of first going to God. This same thing happens when it comes to the supernatural. Too often we look to a formula instead of faith. We try to make the fruit show up instead of simply being a branch and allowing the vine to do the work. Essentially, we need to "be" instead of "do."

6 As you therefore have received Christ Jesus the Lord, so walk in Him, 7 rooted and built up in Him and established in the faith, as you have been taught, abounding in it with thanksgiving. 8 Beware lest

anyone cheat you through philosophy and empty deceit, according to the tradition of men, according to the basic principles of the world, and not according to Christ. 9 For in Him dwells all the fullness of the Godhead bodily; 10 and you are complete in Him, who is the head of all principality and power.

Colossians 2:6-10 NKJV

There are millions of people around the world who have received Christ Jesus the Lord, but an extremely small minority of Christians are walking IN HIM. Very few are doing life through Him, rooted in Him and allowing His life to flow through Him. Why? Instead of preaching the Gospel, we have preached traditions, principles, and formulas. We have taken our cues from the world instead of the Holy Spirit and are giving people twenty one steps to a miracle that really involves everything but a relationship with Jesus.

When people try to follow a formula, instead of simply living out of a relationship with Christ, they get cheated out of the success God designed for them to have. Instead of success, they get frustration. You can either do life for Jesus or you can do life through Jesus. When you do life for Jesus, you can have great intentions, but not produce any results.

I choose to do the latter. I choose to do life through Jesus and get results just like Jesus! Don't ever forget Acts 17:28 that says, "We live and move and have our being in Him!" The formula for experiencing the supernatural is simple: be a branch and stay connected to the Vine.

Just as Jesus said He could do nothing without the Father, He is letting us know we can do nothing without Him. So, this should tell us if fruit isn't being produced, it is simply because we are endeavoring to do it outside of our union with Christ.

We can see this truth again in Galatians 2.

20 I have been crucified with Christ; it is no longer I who live, but Christ lives in me; and the life which I now live in the flesh I live by faith in the Son of God, who loved me and gave Himself for me. 21 I do not set aside the grace of God...

Galatians 2:20-21 NKJV

If you don't do life through Jesus, you set aside the grace of God and therefore, you will not produce fruit. We are a spirit, united to the King of the supernatural and because of our union, the supernatural will naturally manifest in our life.

This is why it's so important to understand the reality of being a spirit being and our union with Christ. When we do so, we stop looking to outside sources and the natural things in life to try and get the supernatural to happen.

Remember the deal with Samson? The supernatural occurred in his life not because of a feeling, but because of faith in what he knew was available. When you know the power of God is available, then the power of God will flow and the supernatural will be natural.

Chapter 8
A Possessor Of Life

7 And the Lord God formed man of the dust of the ground, and breathed into his nostrils the breath of life; and man became a living being.

Genesis 2:7 NKJV

God started out creation by creating a body and putting His life inside of man's spirit and then putting that spirit into the body. Adam didn't become alive until he received of God's life, so this shows us God made us to be possessors of His life. When Adam sinned, that is when he died spiritually and lost the life of God.

You see, that is what Satan was after: the life of God. Satan doesn't care about man, but he does care about what God put into man. Satan knew if he could get the life of God out of man, man wouldn't be a threat to him.

1 Now the serpent was more cunning than any beast of the field which the Lord God had made. And he said to the woman, "Has God indeed said, 'You shall not eat of every tree of the garden'?" 2 And the woman said to the serpent, "We may eat the fruit of the trees of the garden; 3 but of the fruit of the tree which is in the midst of the garden, God has said, 'You shall not eat it, nor shall you touch it, lest you die.'" 4 Then the serpent said to the woman, "You will not surely die. 5 For God knows that in the day you eat of it your eyes will be opened, and you will be like God, knowing good and evil." 6 So when the woman saw that the tree was good for food, that it was pleasant to the eyes, and a tree desirable to make one wise, she took of its fruit and ate. She also gave to her husband with her, and he ate. 7 Then the eyes of both of them were opened, and they knew that they were naked; and they sewed fig leaves together and made themselves coverings.

Genesis 3:1-7 NKJV

This was the ultimate deception. Notice in verse 4 and 5 what Satan says. He said, "If you do this, you will be like God." The reason it was a deception is because Adam and Eve were already like God in the fact they were filled with His very life and nature. Satan couldn't take the life of God away from them so he had to deceive them.

Now this is very important. The Bible tells us that Eve was deceived, but Adam wasn't. What it came down to was Adam knew about his union with God and Eve didn't. Eve didn't know she was filled with God's life; otherwise Satan's line on her wouldn't have worked. Get this please: she wanted what she already had! The sad part is she didn't know what she had and therefore, she looked to natural means to try and produce a spiritual result. She was naturally supernatural and didn't know it!

Thankfully, God is a genius and He had plan already in place to get the life of God back into mankind and it was through His wonderful Son Jesus.

4 In Him was life, and the life was the light of men.
John 1:4 NKJV

The word *life* is the Greek word *zoe* which means the absolute fullness of life that belongs to God.[1] Jesus was a possessor of the life of God or what we more commonly refer to as eternal life or abundant life. A key factor in Jesus life was not only did He possess the life of God, He knew he possessed the life of God. When you know what you have, then you can do something with it.

10 The thief does not come except to steal, and to kill, and to destroy. I have come that they may have life, and that they may have it more abundantly.

John 10:10 NKJV

The same word *life* in John 5:26 is used in John 10:10. In its usage, Jesus is saying the same thing; He possesses it and wants to give it away. Not only did Jesus say He came to give life away, Jesus says He came so we could have life. The phrase *they might have* is from the Greek tense that means to have and to continually possess.[2]

Jesus was a possessor of the life of God and He came so we could be a possessor of the life of God; this life was something we would have and continually possess! In reality, Jesus was simply trying to give humanity back what was stolen in the Garden of Eden. It's why Jesus is referred to as the second Adam! The same life God put into Adam was the same life God put into Jesus and it's the same life Jesus came to put into you!

How We Get The Life Of God

So how do we get the life of God? You get connected to the Vine; you get connected to Jesus because John 1:4 tells us that in Jesus is life . Basically, it all begins with salvation.

17 Therefore, if anyone is in Christ, he is a new creation; old things have passed away; behold, all things have become new.

2 Corinthians 5:17 NKJV

When you got in Christ, you got in His life. You began to share of what He possessed; what was flowing in the Vine was now flowing through you. Just as life flows from the vine to the branches, so life flows from Jesus to us.

11 And this is the testimony: that God has given us eternal life, and this life is in His Son. 12 He who has the Son has life; he who does not have the Son of God does not have life.

1 John 5:11-12 NKJV

Once you accept Christ as your Lord and Savior and receive salvation, you receive of God's life. If you have the Son, you have His life! You don't have to work to get it. You don't have to try and be good enough to get it. All you have to do is get connected to the Vine! All you have to do is get united to Jesus! Once that happens, things begin to happen. The supernatural should start becoming natural because God just got into you!

South Padre Island

In March of 1998, I had an experience that forever changed my outlook on salvation. I was in college and went with some of my friends in the Baptist Student Union on a mission trip to South Padre Island. Now it may not sound like the typical mission trip destination, but if you have seen spring break at South Padre Island, it's blatantly obvious there are a lot of people who need Jesus!

Because all the spring breakers were there to basically get wasted and party hard, we were providing free van rides for them from the clubs to their hotel rooms so they wouldn't be drinking and driving. We were also providing free pancake breakfasts for anyone that wanted some breakfast; it was a wonderful opportunity to show them the love of Christ and establish some rapport with them. We had also set up a coffee house on the main road in town to give them a place to sober up a little bit during the evenings.

One night, several of us were out on the streets telling people about Jesus. After a few hours, I walked to the corner of our coffee house and was waiting for a van ride to return to my hotel. As I was standing there, this young guy stumbled into me and fell to the ground. He was so drunk he couldn't get back up; he was just sitting there in the street.

Well, I picked him up and helped him walk down to our coffee shop. Once we arrived, I sat him down at a table and we began to talk. His speech was slurred and he was doing good just to sit in his chair, but we were able to talk about Jesus. I asked him if he wanted to make Jesus his Lord and Savior to which the young man replied, "Yes." So we closed our eyes and I had him repeat a prayer.

God is my witness that as soon as I opened my eyes, the young man exclaimed, "Whoa!" He said, "It feels like a huge pack of weight was taken off my back. I feel great." Friend, this young man was completely sober! Within 15 minutes of stumbling into me, falling on the ground and dragging him over to the coffee shop, he was completely sober. He didn't have any coffee; all he did was receive Jesus!

The life of God in Jesus flowed into that man's spirit, which in turn flowed into His body and completely set the man free. The young man didn't try to make it happen. He didn't work to manifest the supernatural; it was simply a by-product of becoming a possessor of the life of God.

Now I didn't know much back then, but I was absolutely amazed at the sudden transformation. Looking back, I understand exactly what happened. The guy was born again and received eternal life.

Eternal Life Is More Than Just The Golden Ticket To Heaven

13 These things I have written to you who believe in the name of the Son of God, that you may know that you have eternal life, and that you may continue to believe in the name of the Son of God.

1 John 5:13 NKJV

When we hear about receiving eternal life, most of us instantly think about living in Heaven forever, but that is not what eternal life is all about. Thank God for Heaven, but Jesus didn't die for you to have a destination; Jesus died so you could have a relationship and therefore partake of the life of God! Yes, I'm grateful for Heaven and grateful that Hell is not in my destiny, but I'm more thankful that because of Jesus, I share in that life! Because I am a possessor of the life of God, I can start partaking of that life right now!

I don't have to wait until I get to Heaven to experience His life. Notice the Apostle John tells us that because we believe in Jesus, we have eternal life; he isn't writing to tell us of something we will possess when we leave the earth. John is writing to tell us of what we possess RIGHT NOW!

He isn't talking about a destination; God is talking about a way of life. Jesus didn't say He came so we could go somewhere; Jesus came so we could have something – the life of God. It's not so much about going somewhere, but about being something full of Someone.

Do you understand now why Satan did what he did with Eve? Satan wasn't concerned about our destination. In the beginning, the plan wasn't for Adam to leave the Earth and go to Heaven; Adam's responsibility was to make Earth like Heaven. When we possess the life of God, it puts us in a position of being a champion over Satan and manifesting Heaven on Earth. As a possessor of the life of God, you are potentially dangerous to Satan.

Satan doesn't care about our destination; he cares about what we possess.

Now I say potentially on purpose, because you are not a viable threat to Satan if you don't know what you have. It is why in most of the New Testament, God is telling us who we are in Christ and what we have in Christ. *There isn't much about what we will possess, but there is a whole lot about what we do possess and God needs us to know what we possess!*

It's the reason Satan is constantly bombarding you with thoughts of inadequacy and insufficiency. It's why Satan endeavors to get you to work to obtain what Jesus already provided because as long as you are working to get something, you will never use what Jesus provided.

Chapter 9
Releasing The Life Of God

Can you give something away that you don't have? Absolutely not. I can't give you a car if I don't have one to give, but if I own a car free and clear and it's in my possession, I can give it to whoever I want whenever I want. Jesus said the same thing about the life of God.

> **21 For just as the Father gives life to those he raises from the dead, so the Son gives life to anyone he wants.**
> **John 5:21 NLT**

Jesus not only knew He possessed the life of God, He also knew He could give it away. When you know you possess something, it puts you in a unique position of being able to help someone when they are in need of what you have. If I have $100 and a friend was in need of $100, I can give it to them. Not only that, I don't have to ask anyone's permission to do so. Why? Because it is mine and I can do what I want with it.

If You Knew The Gift Of God

This right here is why you'll never find Jesus praying for God to heal someone. It is why you always see Jesus respond in faith. Why? Because Jesus knew He had the solution; Jesus was a possessor of the life of God. When you know who you are and what you possess, you become an asset to God.

5 So He came to a city of Samaria which is called Sychar, near the plot of ground that Jacob gave to his son Joseph. 6 Now Jacob's well was there. Jesus therefore, being wearied from His journey, sat thus by the well. It was about the sixth hour. 7 A woman of Samaria came to draw water. Jesus said to her, "Give Me a drink." 8 For His disciples had gone away into the city to buy food. 9 Then the woman of Samaria said to Him, "How is it that You, being a Jew, ask a drink from me, a Samaritan woman?" For Jews have no dealings with Samaritans. 10 Jesus answered and said to her,

"If you knew the gift of God, and who it is who says to you, 'Give Me a drink,' you would have asked Him, and He would have given you living water."

John 4:5-10 NKJV

Do you see Jesus response to the woman? There are two pieces I want you to see. In verse 10, Jesus said, "If you knew the gift of God." Jesus knew who He was; Jesus knew He was a gift of God. Just like Jesus, if you have received eternal life, you are a gift of God to the world too. Do you know what you do with a gift? You open it up and enjoy what is inside the package! *Inside of your spirit is the very life of Almighty God that can heal every sickness, destroy every cancer, raise up the dead and pull a person out of the very grips of Hell.*

Notice the latter part of Jesus statement. Jesus said to her, "I would have given you living water." Jesus knew what He possessed and He knew He could give it away.

Not only could Jesus release the life of God by faith, people could receive it from Jesus by faith. After people began to see Jesus ministry, they started to figure out there was something special about Him. City after city began to find out that the power of God was flowing out of Jesus and therefore, multitudes were flocking to Him.

17 And He came down with them and stood on a level place with a crowd of His disciples and a great multitude of people from all Judea and Jerusalem, and from the seacoast of Tyre and Sidon, who came to hear Him and be healed of their diseases, 18 as well as those who were tormented with unclean spirits. And they were healed. 19 And the whole multitude sought to touch Him, for power went out from Him and healed them all.

Luke 6:17-19 NKJV

Why were the multitudes of people trying to touch Jesus? Power was going out of Him and healing people! Where was that power coming from? It was the life of God within His spirit and by faith, people were reaching out and getting a hold of God's life for their bodies.

This wasn't the only time something like this was recorded in the Bible. A familiar story for many is the woman with the issue of blood.

24 Jesus went with him, and all the people followed, crowding around him. 25 A woman in the crowd had suffered for twelve years with constant bleeding. 26

She had suffered a great deal from many doctors, and over the years she had spent everything she had to pay them, but she had gotten no better. In fact, she had gotten worse. 27 She had heard about Jesus, so she came up behind him through the crowd and touched his robe. 28 For she thought to herself, "If I can just touch his robe, I will be healed." 29 Immediately the bleeding stopped, and she could feel in her body that she had been healed of her terrible condition. 30 Jesus realized at once that healing power had gone out from him, so he turned around in the crowd and asked, "Who touched my robe?" 31 His disciples said to him, "Look at this crowd pressing around you. How can you ask, 'Who touched me?'" 32 But he kept on looking around to see who had done it. 33 Then the frightened woman, trembling at the realization of what had happened to her, came and fell to her knees in front of him and told him what she had done. 34 And he said to her, "Daughter, your faith has made you well. Go in peace. Your suffering is over."

Mark 5:24-34 NLT

When most Christians and ministers read this story, they read it from the perspective of the woman; however, I want you to read it from the perspective of Jesus. Most read it as a way to get healed; *I want you to read it as a way to get people healed.*

Release The Power

Jesus said he felt power go out of where? Out of him! For the power to go out of Him, it had to be in Him. This my friend is why Jesus told us to lay hands on the sick. We are possessors of the life and power of God and it can be released by faith.

We also see in Luke 6 and Mark 5 that the life of God is transferable. The multitudes touched Him and the power flowed out of Him. The woman with the issue of blood simply touched his clothes and the life of God went out of Jesus and into her body instantly healing her. We see a similar situation with the Apostle Paul in Acts 19.

11 Now God worked unusual miracles by the hands of Paul, 12 so that even handkerchiefs or aprons were brought from his body to the sick, and the diseases left them and the evil spirits went out of them.

Acts 19:11-12 NKJV

Cloth Containers

In some church circles like the ones I run in, people bring cloths or even stuffed animals for us to lay hands on and then take back to the sick. The reason being is because the life of God can be released into cloth. Why cloth? I don't know except for that God set it up that way. There is Scripture for it and because of that, I'll take it and run with it! These cloths were touching Paul's body and then being taken to the sick. Just like Jesus clothes soaked up the life of God from His body, the cloths from Paul's body were absorbing the power of God as well. These cloths were containers of the power of God and when people touched them in faith, that power was released.

Several years ago, there was a two year time span when we were seeing lots and lots of cancers healed and many of them were taking place through us laying hands on cloths. I'll never forget one lady who lived in Oklahoma City. She had stage 3 breast cancer and had requested us to lay hands on a cloth and send to her. Well, that next Sunday morning we had several of our church people impart the life of God into that cloth and then we sent it to Oklahoma City. Within a few weeks, we received a letter from her stating that at her most recent exam, she received a clean bill of health from her doctor! Around the same time, there was a man who had been diagnosed with lymphoma. I particularly remember this one because right before we laid hands on the cloth, my right hand began to burn like someone put a hot coal in it. We imparted the power of God into that cloth and sent it to the man with lymphoma. About two weeks later, we received word that he was cancer free! Praise God!

When You Know, It Will Flow

When you know what you possess, you can give it away. When you know, it will flow! You don't have to work up anything or have any special music. All you have to do is know what you have and release it by faith. The life of God knows what to do and knows where to go, but it will never get there unless you release it.

Are you starting to see how naturally supernatural you are? The more you understand your union with Christ, the more exciting life becomes!

Chapter 10

Supernatural Equipment

12 Most assuredly, I say to you, he who believes in Me, the works that I do he will do also; and greater works than these he will do, because I go to My Father.

John 14:12 NKJV

This statement by Jesus ignited my pursuit of experiencing the power of God. Ever since I was nineteen years old, I have yearned to experience God; not just hear about Him, but experience Him and be used by Him. In John 14:12, Jesus made a statement which when you take it at face value, it sets a crossroad before you. You either believe it and run with it or do like the majority of Christians do and explain it away.

Well, I chose to believe that what Jesus said was true and as a result, my years of ministry have not been in just teaching, but also experiencing.

The Works Of Jesus

Before we go any further, let's define what Jesus was talking about when He said "works." I've heard lots of preachers say Jesus was talking about feeding the hungry, clothing the naked and housing the homeless; in other words, a ministry to the poor. Granted, Jesus did do these things and they are good things for us to do, but Jesus was not talking about a social welfare system here. If we want to find the answer, all we have to do is look at Scripture.

20 For the Father loves the Son and shows him everything he is doing. In fact, the Father will show him how to do even greater works than healing this man. Then you will truly be astonished.

John 5:20 NLT

I absolutely love this statement. In this, you not only see Jesus extremely high expectation to experience more of the supernatural, but we also begin to get a glimpse of what

Jesus is truly referring to when he talks about "doing the works." What were the "works" in relation to? The "works" were in relation to Jesus healing the paralyzed man that was dropped through a roof during His meeting. Jesus is definitely talking about the supernatural here.

> **35 John was like a burning and shining lamp, and you were excited for a while about his message. 36 But I have a greater witness than John—my teachings and my miracles. The Father gave me these works to accomplish, and they prove that he sent me.**
>
> **John 5:35-36 NLT**

Again, Jesus talks about the works and refers to the miraculous. Notice also Jesus said He had a greater witness than John the Baptist. What was the witness? The supernatural! Anyone saved or unsaved can give someone food or a jacket, but it takes the power of God to bring about healing in a person's body.

> **25 Jesus replied, "I have already told you, and you don't believe me. The proof is the work I do in my Father's name. 26 But you don't believe me because you are not my sheep. 27 My sheep listen to my voice; I know them, and they follow me. 28 I give them eternal life,**

and they will never perish. No one can snatch them away from me, 29 for my Father has given them to me, and he is more powerful than anyone else. No one can snatch them from the Father's hand. 30 The Father and I are one." 31 Once again the people picked up stones to kill him. 32 Jesus said, "At my Father's direction I have done many good works. For which one are you going to stone me?" 33 They replied, "We're stoning you not for any good work, but for blasphemy! You, a mere man, claim to be God." 34 Jesus replied, "It is written in your own Scriptures that God said to certain leaders of the people, 'I say, you are gods!' 35 And you know that the Scriptures cannot be altered. So if those people who received God's message were called 'gods,' 36 why do you call it blasphemy when I say, 'I am the Son of God'? After all, the Father set me apart and sent me into the world. 37 Don't believe me unless I carry out my Father's work. 38 But if I do his work, believe in the evidence of the miraculous works I have done, even if you don't believe me. Then you will know and understand that the Father is in me, and I am in the Father." 39 Once again they tried to arrest him, but he got away and left them. 40 He went beyond the Jordan River near the place where John was first baptizing and stayed there awhile. 41 And

many followed him. "John didn't perform miraculous signs," they remarked to one another, "but everything he said about this man has come true." 42 And many who were there believed in Jesus.

John 10:25-42 NLT

In John 10, Jesus is dealing with the Pharisees. At this point, they are pretty ticked off with Jesus, but then Jesus puts them in their place and continues talking about the works of the Father. In this passage of Scripture, Jesus refers to the works of the Father five times and the entire time, Jesus is referring to the supernatural. Notice in verse 38, Jesus specifically says the miraculous works are the works of God.

Tell What You've Seen And Heard

So if it isn't clear yet, it's about to get blatantly clear. In Luke 7, Jesus has a conversation with the disciples of John the Baptist and it flat out lets us know what Jesus was all about.

18 The disciples of John the Baptist told John about everything Jesus was doing. So John called for two of

his disciples, 19 and he sent them to the Lord to ask him, "Are you the Messiah we've been expecting, or should we keep looking for someone else?" 20 John's two disciples found Jesus and said to him, "John the Baptist sent us to ask, 'Are you the Messiah we've been expecting, or should we keep looking for someone else?'" 21 At that very time, Jesus cured many people of their diseases, illnesses, and evil spirits, and he restored sight to many who were blind. 22 Then he told John's disciples, "Go back to John and tell him what you have seen and heard—the blind see, the lame walk, the lepers are cured, the deaf hear, the dead are raised to life, and the Good News is being preached to the poor.

Luke 7:19-22 NLT

Here is John the Baptist, the man who first announced Jesus as the Messiah. As some time goes by, even John starts wondering if Jesus really is the Messiah and sends his disciples to Jesus. I absolutely love the way Jesus responds. First, Jesus doesn't respond with words, but with action. Jesus got to working the works! He healed people of their diseases, cast out evil spirits and healed many of the blind. Jesus then looks at John's disciples and says, "Go tell John what you have seen and heard."

Right here Jesus declares Himself to be a man among boys. Most ministers today would simply say, "Go tell John what you have heard" because they don't have any stories of the supernatural; all they have is a good five point sermon.

Check out what Jesus wants them to report back to John. It wasn't that there were multitudes of people following Jesus, it wasn't that Jesus was a great speaker and it wasn't that Jesus took care of the poor. Those were things that anyone could do. No, Jesus said, "Go tell John the blind see, the lame walk, the lepers are cured, the deaf hear, the dead are raised to life and the Good News is preached to the poor."

Are you starting to see it? Just in case you need a little bit more help, look at what happened right before John's disciples first told him about what Jesus was doing.

11 Soon afterward Jesus went with his disciples to the village of Nain, and a large crowd followed him. 12 A funeral procession was coming out as he approached the village gate. The young man who had died was a widow's only son, and a large crowd from the village was with her. 13 When the Lord saw her, his heart

overflowed with compassion. "Don't cry!" he said. 14 Then he walked over to the coffin and touched it, and the bearers stopped. "Young man," he said, "I tell you, get up." 15 Then the dead boy sat up and began to talk! And Jesus gave him back to his mother. 16 Great fear swept the crowd, and they praised God, saying, "A mighty prophet has risen among us," and "God has visited his people today." 17 And the news about Jesus spread throughout Judea and the surrounding countryside.

Luke 7:11-17 NLT

Jesus had just raised a young man from the dead during the funeral procession – that will certainly get people's attention! The news of this event spread all throughout the land. Not only were the religious leaders hearing and seeing everything Jesus was doing, so were John the Baptist's disciples. They didn't go back to John and tell him about the social outreaches Jesus was doing. Among other miraculous works, they told him about the dead man being raised.

Almost every time Jesus refers to the works of the Father, Jesus is talking about the supernatural power of God and most of the time it was specifically about healing. The works of Jesus were supernatural works!

The Same Works

So now that we have established what the works are, let's look back at Jesus statement in John 14.

12 Most assuredly, I say to you, he who believes in Me, the works that I do he will do also; and greater works than these he will do, because I go to My Father.

John 14:12 NKJV

Jesus tells us that whoever believes in Him will do the same works He did and even greater works. Notice Jesus doesn't specify that the people who will do the miracles will be the fivefold ministry folks. Jesus didn't say it would be the apostle, prophet, pastor, evangelist and teacher who would do the miracles. Jesus didn't say anything about degrees or conferred titles. Jesus didn't say you had to be the bishop and senior founding pastor of the Running With Jesus Apostolic Pentecostal Assembly of Baptist Churches! Jesus made it plain and simple; the only title Jesus mentioned was that of a believer. *So if you believe in Jesus as your Lord and Savior, Jesus is talking about you!*

Now that you can't weasel your way out of this promise, let's get down to business. If you are going to do the same works as Jesus – if you are going to see the lame walk, the blind see, the deaf hear, the dead raised, demons cast out and the diseased cured – won't you at least need the very same equipment as Jesus?

The Same Equipment

Do you think you are capable of doing what Jesus did without the very same equipment? No way is that happening! If we are going to do what Jesus did, at the very least, we must have the same equipment that Jesus had. So check this out: not only is it true that we need the same equipment Jesus had, Jesus even confirms this for us.

18 As You sent Me into the world, I also have sent them into the world.

John 17:18 NKJV

John 17 is one of my favorite chapters in the Bible. Here we find Jesus praying in the Garden of Gethsemane and He begins to reveal phenomenal truths about our union with Him and the Father. In verse 18, Jesus blows holes in our religious teaching of lack and says, "In the same way the Father sent Me into the world, I'm sending them." Do you think God sent Jesus from Heaven to this earth without the necessary equipment? That's a pretty dumb question isn't it. Well then, let me ask you another question. Do you think Jesus would send you into the world without the necessary equipment? I don't think so.

It would be absolutely unfair and unjust for Jesus to send us into the world to represent Him and produce results just like Him without the same equipment. This would be like me having a professional lawn care service with various commercial grade equipment and then hiring you to take care of my clients. I then send you out to a property requiring an acre of grass to be cut, bushes to be shaped and pathways to be edged – and expected you to do it only with some scissors and a broom and get the same results as me. How stupid is that? I would be off my rocker to think it would be possible and you would probably be looking at me thinking I must have lost my mind!

This scenario is crazy, but it's exactly the way we look at Jesus and the commission He has given us. He sent us into the world to represent Him, but instead of believing we could get the job done, we start questioning our equipment by getting over into the feelings realm again. So we start praying for more faith, more anointing, more power, more righteousness, blah, blah, blah, blah, blah. Jesus sent you and I into the world packing some serious heat! We've got all the goods we need to fulfill what Jesus called us to do! For you to begin to question this truth would be to question your union with Christ.

17 As He is, so are we in this world.

1 John 4:17 NKJV

How are we in this world? As Jesus is RIGHT NOW. Do you think Jesus is seated at God's right hand lacking in any area? I would have a hard time seeing Jesus crying out to God, "I don't have enough to get the job done." On the contrary, Jesus is complete, lacking nothing. Because of our union with Christ, God has graced us with the equipment needed to get the job done just as if He were doing it Himself. Remember, Jesus is the Vine and we are the branches. As He is in spirit, so are we. We are one spirit with the Lord; therefore, whatever is flowing through Him is flowing through us. He is the Head of the Church and we are the body; we are vitally connected so that God's supernatural miraculous power can be manifest on the earth.

Jesus was our standard. In the same way He could hear from God, we can hear from God. In the same way Jesus could work the miraculous, we can work the miraculous. Why? We have the same equipment because we are united with Christ; so, let's take a look at some of this equipment.

Chapter 11
The Faith Of God

22 And the fruit of the Spirit is: Love, joy, peace, long-suffering, kindness, goodness, faith...

Galatians 5:22 KJV

One of the statements I hear the most from Christians is "I just don't have enough faith." Friend, if you have accepted Jesus as your Lord and Savior, you not only have the faith that can move mountains, you have the faith that made mountains because God gave you His faith.

The fruit of the Spirit are traits of God that are imparted to us at the new birth. When you were born again, you took on God's genetics! When you accepted Jesus as your Lord and Savior, the old you died and the new you was united with Christ. He is the Vine and you are the branches, so whatever is flowing through Him is flowing through you.

We have no problem accepting as truth that we have and can operate in God's peace, joy, love, patience, etc., but when it comes to God's faith, that's when you hear the car tires come to a screeching halt!

It's always interesting that the areas Satan battles against the most are the areas that usually provide us the way of victory. Think about the issue of faith. How important is faith to the Christian?

1. We walk by faith. (2 Corinthians 5:7)

2. We live by faith. (Hebrews 10:38)

3. We receive the promises by faith. (Hebrews 6:12)

4. We can't please God without faith. (Hebrews 11:6)

5. We are justified by faith. (Romans 5:1)

Do you think God would require us to do these things without giving us what was needed? God never has put us in a position to fulfill His commands without His grace giving us the equipment. In the same measure we have been given God's love to flood our entire being, God has given us His faith to believe like Him, live like Him, walk like Him and receive like Him, thus putting a big smile on His face and pleasing Him.

How could you possibly walk in the supernatural like Jesus without having the same measure of faith? It wouldn't be possible! Because we understand that, we've put a major focus on getting enough faith so we can do what God needs us to do, but of course, if you base your faith on your feelings, you will never have enough faith. If you base your faith on your experiences, you will never have enough faith either.

Jesus Faith

The only way you will have enough faith is when you start using Jesus faith. When you start living through Him, His faith naturally begins to flow through you.

6 As you therefore have received Christ Jesus the Lord, so walk in Him, 7 rooted and built up in Him and established in the faith, as you have been taught, abounding in it with thanksgiving. 8 Beware lest anyone cheat you through philosophy and empty

deceit, according to the tradition of men, according to the basic principles of the world, and not according to Christ. 9 For in Him dwells all the fullness of the Godhead bodily; 10 and you are complete in Him, who is the head of all principality and power.

Colossians 2:6-10 NKJV

When we accepted Christ, we became complete; nothing missing and nothing broken! Jesus is the fullness of the Godhead bodily and we are complete in Him. How could you possibly not have enough faith when He has given you His faith?

Use What You Have

Jesus never had faith failures nor a lack of faith because His faith wasn't in His faith; His faith was in His union with God. This is why you never see Jesus teaching the disciples how to get more faith; instead, Jesus always taught them to use what they had.

1 One day Jesus said to his disciples, "There will always be temptations to sin, but what sorrow awaits the person who does the tempting! 2 It would be better to

be thrown into the sea with a millstone hung around your neck than to cause one of these little ones to fall into sin. 3 So watch yourselves! "If another believer sins, rebuke that person; then if there is repentance, forgive. 4 Even if that person wrongs you seven times a day and each time turns again and asks forgiveness, you must forgive." 5 The apostles said to the Lord, "Show us how to increase our faith." 6 The Lord answered, "If you had faith even as small as a mustard seed, you could say to this mulberry tree, 'May you be uprooted and thrown into the sea,' and it would obey you!

Luke 17:1-6 NLT

The only time Jesus was asked by the disciples about getting more faith is found here in Luke 17 when Jesus was teaching them about forgiveness. You would think Jesus would have taken advantage of this prime teaching opportunity to teach the disciples how to get more faith wouldn't you? After all, they were in training for ministry! Instead, Jesus disregards their statement. Rather than teach them how to get more faith, Jesus simply tells them to use what they have.

Now it's obvious that some people use their faith in a

greater way than others; after all, we see Jesus using His faith in spectacular ways and in similar situations, we see the disciples struggle.

22 One day Jesus said to his disciples, "Let's cross to the other side of the lake." So they got into a boat and started out. 23 As they sailed across, Jesus settled down for a nap. But soon a fierce storm came down on the lake. The boat was filling with water, and they were in real danger. 24 The disciples went and woke him up, shouting, "Master, Master, we're going to drown!" When Jesus woke up, he rebuked the wind and the raging waves. Suddenly the storm stopped and all was calm. 25 Then he asked them, "Where is your faith?"

Luke 8:22-25 NLT

Here is a great example of Jesus faith versus the disciple's faith. Jesus calms the storm and then rebukes the disciples for basically not taking care of business themselves. Jesus expected them to do it, but they didn't. Notice Jesus didn't say, "Well boys, if you had enough faith, you could have calmed the storm; I know you aren't there yet, so don't worry about it." No, Jesus expected them to do something about it because they were capable of doing so.

22 Immediately Jesus made His disciples get into the boat and go before Him to the other side, while He sent the multitudes away. 23 And when He had sent the multitudes away, He went up on the mountain by Himself to pray. Now when evening came, He was alone there. 24 But the boat was now in the middle of the sea, tossed by the waves, for the wind was contrary. 25 Now in the fourth watch of the night Jesus went to them, walking on the sea. 26 And when the disciples saw Him walking on the sea, they were troubled, saying, "It is a ghost!" And they cried out for fear. 27 But immediately Jesus spoke to them, saying, "Be of good cheer! It is I; do not be afraid." 28 And Peter answered Him and said, "Lord, if it is You, command me to come to You on the water." 29 So He said, "Come." And when Peter had come down out of the boat, he walked on the water to go to Jesus. 30 But when he saw that the wind was boisterous, he was afraid; and beginning to sink he cried out, saying, "Lord, save me!" 31 And immediately Jesus stretched out His hand and caught him, and said to him, "O you of little faith, why did you doubt?" 32 And when they got into the boat, the wind ceased.

Matthew 14:22-32 NKJV

I think it would be safe to say that from most people's perspective, it would take some crazy faith to walk on the water! So many times Peter gets chided because of the latter part of the story, but have you really ever paid attention to the first part of the story? This guy stepped out of the boat and started walking on the water! Do you realize how phenomenal that was?

Would you agree that it took faith to walk on the water? I would definitely say "Yes!" In your opinion, would it have taken some super-duper-alley–ooper-faith to walk on the water? I would say "Yes" as well. I mean, out of every supernatural miracle I have read in the Gospels, for me, walking on the water wins the gold! Not only did Jesus walk on the water, but Peter walked on the water too – that is some big time faith.

Little Faith, Big Faith

So Peter exercised some superman faith walking on the water and then made a mistake; he stopped focusing on Jesus and started focusing on the wind and waves. When Peter did that, he sunk. Jesus, in His love, grabbed him and pulled him back to the surface. Then Jesus says, "Peter, you have such little faith." Wait a minute! Little faith? Peter just walked on the water! Although, Jesus isn't interested in us starting something; He wants us to finish. Jesus is very big on results and you don't get results by having roller coaster faith.

Jesus wasn't really questioning if Peter had faith or not; the amount was not the issue. Obviously, Peter had more than enough faith because again – the dude walked on water! This wasn't an equipment problem; this was an awareness **Faith comes naturally when you are aware of Jesus.** problem. Peter's faith was fine as long as he was aware of Jesus; Peter's faith took a nose dive when he became more aware of the circumstances. Peter's faith only became little when he became more aware of natural things.

I also want you to notice that Peter didn't follow a faith formula before he experienced the supernatural on the water. He didn't go through his handbook of miracles or "5 steps of releasing your faith" pamphlet; all Peter did was have his eyes on Jesus. Friend, faith comes naturally when you are aware of Jesus. When you are very much aware of your union with Him, the supernatural naturally flows and manifests in your life.

Weak Faith, Strong Faith

19 And not being weak in faith, he (Abraham) did not consider his own body, already dead (since he was about a hundred years old), and the deadness of Sarah's womb. 20 He did not waver at the promise of God through unbelief, but was strengthened in faith, giving glory to God, 21 and being fully convinced that what He had promised He was also able to perform.

Romans 4:19-21 NKJV

God promised Abraham that he and Sarah would have a child together; the biggest hurdle was that Abraham and Sarah were very old and Sarah was way past her child bearing years. However, the Bible tells us Abraham was not weak in faith. Why? Abraham wasn't focused on his body; he was focused on God.

Just like Peter, Abraham was strong in faith because his eyes were not on the problem, but on the greatness of God. The Bible also tells us Abraham became even stronger in faith as He praised God. So, the difference between strong faith, weak faith, big faith and little faith is not in the amount; it's in the focus. What are you focused on? What are you more aware of?

We Have An Awareness Problem

As a believer, we do not have a faith problem; we simply have an awareness problem. Most of us do not know what we have and who we have been united with through salvation. You can do faith through a formula and it will only lead to frustration or you can do faith through fellowship and it will lead to supernatural results. Faith from a formula is strenuous; faith from a fellowship is effortless.

I guarantee Peter wasn't walking on the water confessing "I believe I receive, I believe I receive." Peter wasn't trying to work something! Peter wasn't trying to make sure he had heard enough Scripture and made enough confessions before he stepped out on the water and manifested the supernatural. Peter wasn't checking to see if he was in faith or if he had any unforgiveness in his life; Peter was just fully aware of Jesus. Faith simply rose up out of his heart and caused the supernatural to happen naturally without any effort of his own - that my friend is called faith in His grace.

Looking At You Will Cause You To Fail

When you start focusing on formulas and principles of how to get your faith to work, how to get more faith, and checking to see if you have enough faith or are in faith, you are going to get frustrated. Why? When you start looking at you, you will never be enough and will never have enough.

When you are more focused on your faith than your fellowship with Christ, you will always be frustrated because you will always fail. It will cause you to look at other things to achieve what Jesus already achieved in you; looking at you will lead you out of grace and into works.

Hearing And Hearing And Hearing

Take Romans 10:17. This is such a wonderful Scripture and a freeing Scripture for us, but unfortunately, we have taken it and turned it into a work.

17 So then faith comes by hearing, and hearing by the word of God.

Romans 10:17 NKJV

When you listen to many people quote this, it comes out like this: "Faith comes by hearing and hearing and hearing and hearing the Word of God." Man's natural tendency is to add work to what God has already done. So, we have taken this Scripture and thought we needed to hear and hear and hear and hear and hear so we could get enough faith. The problem is this: when do you know if you have enough?

If faith comes by how much you hear the Word, we should see an entirely different Church in today's world. In the last forty years, we have had the greatest revelation of the Word of God the world has ever experienced. We have the Word being preached on radio, television, internet, CD, DVD, mp3, and podcasts; it's available 24/7 in almost every part of the world.

Faith from a fellowship is effortless.

The Word is being preached all the around the world nonstop and yet we are seeing less and less of the supernatural. Do you know why? Because we have taught people over the years to work from this Scripture and yet we have called it faith.

The Rhema Word

Look at Romans 10:17 again. "Faith comes by hearing and hearing the Word of God." You could essentially read it like this: "Faith comes by hearing the Word of God." The emphasis in this statement is not on the quantity of hearing; *the emphasis in this statement is on the quality of hearing.*

In the Greek, there are two words for *Word*: *logos* and *rhema.* *Logos* means the written Word and *rhema* means the spoken Word. If *logos* was used here, then the emphasis would be on the written Scripture, but it's not; the word *rhema* is used. So the emphasis in Romans 10:17 is not on the written word of God but on the spoken word of God; essentially and emphatically, this verse is about fellowship with God! It's not about knowing Scripture; it's about knowing God!

Our big problem is we are not hearing from God

Faith naturally comes by hearing the spoken Word of God. It's not by repeatedly hearing a Scripture over and over; faith is a natural by-product of a relationship with the Father. We are hearing plenty of Scripture; the problem is we aren't hearing from God. The reason we aren't hearing from God is because we aren't focusing on fellowship; we are focusing on formulas.

It's why we have good hearted Christians reading their devotionals, making their confessions and reading their Bible chapters trying to get enough faith to do what God has called them to do and receive what God has for them to receive. Sadly, for most of them, their Bible reading has turned into a chore instead of a blessing. Instead of the Scripture leading them into a relationship with the Father, it's leading them into a daily job without a vacation.

There is no such thing as true Bible faith outside of your union with Christ. Knowing principles, steps and keys of faith are great; there is nothing wrong with it because they help us to understand how all of this works. The problem comes when we focus more on them than we do on Jesus. When you focus on Jesus, your faith will naturally soar; when you focus on you, your faith will sink to the bottom of the ocean.

When you begin to question your faith, it is your big flashing sign with a blaring horn! This means you took your eyes off of Jesus; you have stepped out of grace and are now operating in works. Get this and get this now: your works will never work to get the supernatural to work. The only way the supernatural works is for you to rest in what Jesus already worked.

You don't need to question your faith. Your equipment is not the issue. Unlike Abraham and Peter, you actually have the faith of God. They weren't saved; they weren't united with Christ and yet look at what they were able to accomplish with lesser equipment! Friend, we have it made. This life we have been called to live is amazing; it is a life in Christ! It is a life where we get to live, move and have our being in Christ! It is a life of faith based on His faith, not our faith. The result of living in Him is living by faith; therefore, living by faith should be natural and effortless.

Focus On His Faith

Don't focus on your faith; focus on His faith. If you could do it on your own, you wouldn't need Jesus! This is why Jesus united you to Him! You became a branch hooked up to the Vine so His supernatural faith and grace could flow through you without any effort of your own. When you accepted Jesus as your Savior, you stepped into a realm free of faith failures. Your faith can't fail because

God's faith can't fail! The faith that created the world is what God imparted to you!

The most important job we have in the area of faith is to develop our fellowship with Jesus. The more aware you are of your union with Him, the greater you will use the faith God has given you without even thinking about it. The more you spend time with Him and hear from Him, the more you will renew your mind to the spiritual realities of redemption; this will automatically result in you increasing the release of God's faith in your life.

Chapter 12
Supernatural Power

19 And [so that you can know and understand] what
is the immeasurable and unlimited and surpassing
greatness of His power in and for us who believe, as
demonstrated in the working of His mighty strength,
20 Which He exerted in Christ when He raised Him
from the dead and seated Him at His [own] right hand
in the heavenly [places].

Ephesians 1:19-20 AMP

In order to do what Jesus did, you must have the same
equipment. In Ephesians, God wants us to emphatically
know what is available for us to use. Do you realize what is

within your spirit? Dead raising power! The same power that raised Jesus from the dead is in you! It's the same power that healed blind Bartimaeus, raised up Lazarus from the dead, caused the lepers to be cleansed and the lame to walk!

That You Would Know

This was the Apostle Paul's prayer for the church. Paul said he prayed continually that they would know the greatness of God's power in us. Notice Paul didn't pray that God would give us the power or that we would receive the power; Paul prayed that we would know what we have!

Unfortunately, most Christians aren't reading what Paul wrote by the Holy Spirit. The majority of Christians are praying for more power because they don't feel like they have enough; do you see how feelings get in the way? If you are going by your feelings, you will most certainly feel like you don't have enough, but if you go by the Bible, you find out you have more than enough!

This is the difference between Christians who live through Jesus and those who live outside of Jesus. When you understand your union with Christ, it's impossible to lack anything – especially the power of God!

11 But if the Spirit of Him who raised Jesus from the dead dwells in you, He who raised Christ from the dead will also give life to your mortal bodies through His Spirit who dwells in you.

Romans 8:11 NKJV

Again, Paul is trying to get across the same information to the Christians. The Holy Spirit, who is the power of God, is the same Spirit and same power that is in you – not going to be in you, but in you right now!

Don't Put Off Your Victory

When we fail to realize what is within us, it will always cause us to put today's victory off until tomorrow. If you don't think you have the necessary equipment to do what Jesus did, then you will either be waiting on God to give it or you will be waiting to get good enough to get it; either way, you will be waiting a long time.

18 For I consider that the sufferings of this present time are not worthy to be compared with the glory which shall be revealed in us. 19 For the earnest expectation

of the creation eagerly waits for the revealing of the sons of God.

Romans 8:18-19 NKJV

When we go to Heaven and the veil is lifted off our eyes, we will see what was in our spirit the entire time we were on earth. For some people, it won't be much of a surprise; for most people, it's going to be like getting hit in the stomach because they will realize the power of Heaven was available yet was wasted. Notice God isn't going to give us glory; God is going to reveal the glory that is already in us. So what exactly is that glory?

4 Therefore we were buried with Him through baptism into death, that just as Christ was raised from the dead by the glory of the Father, even so we also should walk in newness of life.

Romans 6:4 NKJV

The glory of God is the power of God. It was His glory, His power, His Spirit that raised Jesus up from the dead and that dead raising power is in you! It's time we receive such a simple yet profound truth and start walking in it. This power is what allows us to walk a new life; a life full of power and victory. God does not want us to continue in a life of weakness and defeat!

It opens up a life where there is so much of the power of God and life of God within you that nothing on the outside can hinder – no sickness, no disease, no demon, no oppression, no recession, no nothing! We are like a living, breathing nuclear plant. Don't tell me that the dead raising power within your spirit can't knock out a cancer in your body and also demolish a tumor in someone else's body! If it can raise Jesus from the dead, it can heal you of every sickness and disease as well as keep you from ever getting sick again.

27 To them God willed to make known what are the riches of the glory of this mystery among the Gentiles: which is Christ in you, the hope of glory. 28 Him we preach, warning every man and teaching every man in all wisdom, that we may present every man perfect in Christ Jesus. 29 To this end I also labor, striving according to His working which works in me mightily.
Colossians 1:27-29 NKJV

My prayer is just like the Apostle Paul's prayer; I pray you would see this powerful reality of our union with Christ. This has been a mystery for too many for too long, but it's time we take the blinders off of our eyes and grasp what is within us. The mystery of the Gospel is Christ in you and this is why we can expect the glory of God and the power of God to be on display in our lives! We have the Anointed One and His anointing within our spirit. How could we possibly not have enough power to get the job done?

He Is Working In You Mightily

I absolutely love what Paul says in Colossians 1:29. He said, "To this I labor, striving according to His working which works in me mightily." We aren't to be doing life and doing ministry in our own strength and works. We are to do life and ministry according to His power that works in us MIGHTILY!

We shouldn't stand before paralysis any different than we would a fever! They are both from Satan and the power that resides within us not only defeated Satan, but is still more powerful than all of Hell combined. There isn't any devil in Hell that can stand up against a man or women united with Christ. Satan couldn't touch Jesus, so why would you think he could touch you?

Did you ever think about why Satan did what he did? Satan is no match for the power of God; he can't touch the anointing. If Satan touched it, it would be like a mosquito touching a bug zapper! This is why Satan has to work through people to influence them to harm others. Satan had to put the thoughts and intentions into people like Judas and the Pharisees to kill Jesus because mankind was made to handle the power of God.

Remember when we looked at God's creation of mankind? God made Adam's body to be a carrier of His power; God put His life into Adam and Adam received it without any struggle. The woman with the issue of blood had no problem receiving the power of God into her body and Jesus had no problem releasing the power. Why? Our bodies were made to not only receive of God's power but also release God's power; it is simply the way God made us. God made us to be carriers and vessels of supernatural power.

Chapter 13
The Same Spirit

11 But if the Spirit of Him who raised you from the dead dwells in you, He who raised Christ from the dead will also give life to your mortal bodies through His Spirit who dwells in you.

Romans 8:11 NKJV

Have you really ever taken a step back and thought about this? The worker of the power of God is working in you. The Holy Spirit is the power of God! The Holy Spirit is the dispenser of the gifts! Every miracle that happened through Jesus was the result of the Holy Spirit working through Him.

The Holy Spirit who performed the greatest miracle

Heaven, Earth and Hell has ever experienced dwells in you. The same One who went into the pit of Hell, made Jesus spirit alive and lifted Him out of the grave is doing life in you!

The Holy Spirit is seriously the most misunderstood Person of the Trinity. Without the Holy Spirit, the job doesn't get done; He is the workhorse behind all of this. You could look at the Father, Son and Holy Spirit from this perspective to help you understand their roles.

If we were to look at it in the realm of construction, you could view God as the General Contractor, Jesus as the Foreman and the Holy Spirit as the laborer. God gives the orders, Jesus puts the orders into play and the Holy Spirit gets the job done.

Manifesting The Supernatural

Well, let me tell you something! The same Holy Spirit that was within Jesus and causing the supernatural to happen is the same Holy Spirit that is living and working inside of you! The Holy Spirit is in the business of making the supernatural come to pass; that is His job, He is good at it and He has been involved in manifesting the power of God on the earth since its beginning.

> **1 In the beginning God created the heavens and the earth. 2 The earth was formless and empty, and darkness covered the deep waters. And the Spirit of God was hovering over the surface of the waters.**
>
> **Genesis 1:1-2 NLT**

Do you see what the Holy Spirit was doing? As God was recreating the earth, the Holy Spirit was already there ahead of time waiting on God to speak. The Holy Spirit loves to manifest the supernatural. Isn't this exciting? The same Spirit that created the earth lives within you! This is what the Apostle Paul was trying to get across to us!

> **16 Don't you realize that all of you together are the temple of God and that the Spirit of God lives in you?**
>
> **1 Corinthians 3:16 NLT**

> **19 Don't you realize that your body is the temple of the Holy Spirit, who lives in you and was given to you by God? You do not belong to yourself.**
>
> **1 Corinthians 6:19 NLT**

You are the home of the Holy Spirit. Everywhere you go, He is there and if He is there, the power of God is there! There is no limit to His power and therefore, there is no limit to what you can release into this world except for the limits you put into effect by your faith.

There used to be a song we sung growing up in church. The chorus went like this: "More love, more power, more of you in my life." I used to think it was a good song until I started understanding my identity in Christ; then I started realizing that phrase was full of religion!

The Bible says in Romans 5 that the love of God has been shed abroad in my heart by the Holy Spirit! Romans 8:11 tells me the same Spirit that raised Jesus from the dead dwells in me! How could I need more love and power? If I do, then I need to get saved!

When I received salvation, I became wall to wall Holy Spirit. I didn't just get a little of Him; I got all of Him! Remember, if I'm going to do what Jesus did, I need at least the same equipment as Jesus did. If Jesus had the Spirit without measure, then so do I; after all, how am I going to do what Jesus did and get the same results with only a half measure of the Holy Spirit?

The Dispenser Of The Gifts

Over the years, there has been a lot of talk about what gifts are needed for certain miracles or healings to take place. There has also been a lot of emphasis over what gift one person ministers versus another. Now, I am not saying that was has been taught is untrue, but I do believe we have put a greater emphasis on the gifts than God intended. In the entire Bible, there is a portion of one chapter devoted to the gifts of the Spirit which is found in 1 Corinthians 12.

1 Now concerning spiritual gifts, brethren, I do not want you to be ignorant: 2 You know that you were Gentiles, carried away to these dumb idols, however you were led. 3 Therefore I make known to you that no one speaking by the Spirit of God calls Jesus accursed, and no one can say that Jesus is Lord except by the Holy Spirit. 4 There are diversities of gifts, but the same Spirit. 5 There are differences of ministries, but the same Lord. 6 And there are diversities of activities, but it is the same God who works all in all. 7 But the manifestation of the Spirit is given to each one for the profit of all: 8 for to one is given the word of wisdom through the Spirit, to another the word of knowledge through the same Spirit, 9 to another faith

by the same Spirit, to another gifts of healings by the same Spirit, 10 to another the working of miracles, to another prophecy, to another discerning of spirits, to another different kinds of tongues, to another the interpretation of tongues. 11 But one and the same Spirit works all these things, distributing to each one individually as He wills.

1 Corinthians 12:1-11 NKJV

Granted, we all have different calls and anointings on our lives. When we received the baptism of the Holy Spirit, He comes upon us and equips us for ministry. You may not be called to the five fold ministry, but we are all called to the ministry of telling people about Jesus.

We all have different jobs to do and different jobs require different equipment but the dispenser of the equipment is the Holy Spirit. No matter what our anointing is, no matter what part of the Body of Christ we are, we all have the same Spirit operating in our lives. Nowhere are we told that we have to try and make a gift manifest nor are we told we can operate in only certain gifts based on what our title may be.

We should certainly desire the gifts; actually, the Apostle

Paul outright tells us to covet them. But do you realize you can't desire the gifts without desiring a working relationship with the Holy Spirit?

Spirit Conscious

We shouldn't be gift conscious; we need to be Spirit conscious. We are not the distributor of the gifts; the Holy Spirit is the distributor and He will manifest whatever gift is needed at the needed time. I never check to see if a certain gift is in operation before I step out and minister to someone. Sometimes I am aware of a gift and sometimes I am not; either way, I am always aware of the Holy Spirit. If the gifts are distributed as the Holy Spirit wills, then what good does it do me focusing on them?

Let's think about this. What if someone comes to you for healing and you don't have the right gift? How can you help them? Well, you can't and they are going to walk away without the help they needed. Does that sound like the ministry of Jesus? Not even close.

I find it interesting that Jesus didn't teach the disciples about this. Jesus didn't put a focus on the gifts of the Spirit; Jesus put a focus on His union with the Father. When

Jesus sent out His disciples to do ministry, He never once explained what gifts were necessary for each particular job. Jesus simply told them He was giving them power and authority over sickness and disease.

> **1 Then He called His twelve disciples together and gave them power and authority over all demons, and to cure diseases. 2 He sent them to preach the kingdom of God and to heal the sick. 3 And He said to them, "Take nothing for the journey, neither staffs nor bag nor bread nor money; and do not have two tunics apiece. 4 "Whatever house you enter, stay there, and from there depart. 5 And whoever will not receive you, when you go out of that city, shake off the very dust from your feet as a testimony against them." 6 So they departed and went through the towns, preaching the gospel and healing everywhere.**
>
> **Luke 9:1-6 NKJV**

When Jesus sent out the seventy, He said the same thing without any mention of the gifts of the Spirit.

> **1 After these things the Lord appointed seventy others also, and sent them two by two before His face into every city and place where He Himself was about to**

go. 2 Then He said to them, "The harvest truly is great, but the laborers are few; therefore pray the Lord of the harvest to send out laborers into His harvest. 3 Go your way; behold, I send you out as lambs among wolves. 4 Carry neither money bag, knapsack, nor sandals; and greet no one along the road. 5 But whatever house you enter, first say, 'Peace to this house.' 6 And if a son of peace is there, your peace will rest on it; if not, it will return to you. 7 And remain in the same house, eating and drinking such things as they give, for the laborer is worthy of his wages. Do not go from house to house. 8 Whatever city you enter, and they receive you, eat such things as are set before you. 9 And heal the sick there, and say to them, 'The kingdom of God has come near to you.'

Luke 10:1-9 NKJV

After Jesus arose from the dead and appeared to the disciples, He gave what we all know as the Great Commission. Even in this commission, there is no mention of which gifts of the Spirit would be needed.

1 And being assembled together with them, He commanded them not to depart from Jerusalem, but to wait for the Promise of the Father, "which," He said,

"you have heard from Me; 5 for John truly baptized with water, but you shall be baptized with the Holy Spirit not many days from now." 6 Therefore, when they had come together, they asked Him, saying, "Lord, will You at this time restore the kingdom to Israel?" 7 And He said to them, "It is not for you to know times or seasons which the Father has put in His own authority. 8 But you shall receive power when the Holy Spirit has come upon you; and you shall be witnesses to Me in Jerusalem, and in all Judea and Samaria, and to the end of the earth."

Acts 1:4-8 NKJV

In the Great Commission, the emphasis wasn't on the gifts but on the Dispenser of the gifts. I believe wholeheartedly we have sold ourselves short. We have been focusing on a particular apple when we should be focused on the tree. I know that whatever situation is presented to me, because the Holy Spirit is with me, whatever gift that is necessary will manifest. Thank God for the gifts, but I don't focus on the gifts; I focus on the Giver of the gifts.

It is good to know about them and what is available, but nowhere are we told to focus on them. When you begin to focus on a gift, then it puts you in a position of caution and hesitation instead of faith. If before I minister to someone, I start checking to see if a gift is in manifestation, I automatically put myself in a place of questioning the availability of a gift or praying for a gift to manifest. This position isn't going to help me to help others. I can't be doubting, wondering and questioning a gift before I minister to people.

Focusing on the gift is like Peter taking his eyes off of Jesus and focusing on the circumstances. Focusing on the gift makes you take your eyes off of Jesus and put your eyes on yourself. As soon as your eyes get off of Jesus, do you know what happens? You start to sink and at that point, you are of no use to anyone.

Anything that gets your eyes off of Jesus and on to you is religion. Any teaching that causes you to not get the same results as Jesus has some religion in it. You can get religious even with the gifts of the Spirit and I firmly believe many of us have – thus why we haven't been seeing much happening in our churches and special meetings.

Focus on the Giver of the gifts, not the gifts

If we are going to do the same works of Jesus, then we

should get the same results as Jesus. If we aren't seeing the same results, that means we must humble ourselves and find out what part of our belief system needs to be added to, taken away from or modified.

In our ministry, Lacy and I have had blind eyes opened, deaf ears opened, short limbs grow out, tumors dissolve, cancers healed and much, much more. In all of the healings we have personally experienced, not once have I ever either waited for a gift to manifest or checked to see if a gift was present.

Now when it comes to a word of knowledge or word of wisdom, I'll take a moment before I say anything to the individual and check to see if the Holy Spirit has anything He wants me to say. Sometimes there is and sometimes there isn't. If there isn't, then I simply proceed and do what I would normally do unless He tells me otherwise.

In being obedient and stepping out in faith, that is usually when the gifts of the Spirit begin to operate. If the gifts were in operation before I did anything, it would never require faith; however, God is a faith God and He always requires faith - even on the part of the minister!

I know the Holy Spirit is always with me and He is always

ready, willing and able to manifest the supernatural. All He is doing is waiting on the Word of God to be spoken and acted upon and then He's like a cat on a mouse!

If a gift is needed, I know He will take care of it; it's really no concern of mine. I certainly covet the gifts, but I don't focus on the gifts. Be like Jesus; be aware of the Holy Spirit.

In Him, you have everything you need to experience supernatural results just like Jesus. To do what Jesus did, you must have what He had and the good news is: YOU DO! You have the same Spirit that created the world, the same Spirit that worked every miracle in Jesus ministry and the same Spirit that raised Jesus from the dead.

4 You are of God, little children, and have overcome them, because He who is in you is greater than he who is in the world.

1 John 4:4 NKJV

There is nothing more powerful in the world than Who is in you. There is more power in you than in the largest nuclear plant on earth. You are a living, breathing carrier of the power of Heaven; God's power is at your disposal through the Holy Spirit. If you have the Holy Spirit, you have what is needed for any situation.

You weren't created to try and make all of this work. Remember, you are the branch, not the Vine. The Vine does all the work; the Vine makes sure that whatever the branch needs, the branch gets. Our job is to simply stay connected to Jesus. When we do that, whatever supernatural tools are needed will naturally flow through us to minister to the people God has brought across our path.

Chapter 14
Supernatural Authority

Because of our union with Christ, we were restored back to God's original plan for mankind. God's original plan for man was to rule and reign in the earth.

26 Then God said, "Let Us make man in Our image, according to Our likeness; let them have dominion over the fish of the sea, over the birds of the air, and over the cattle, over all the earth and over every creeping thing that creeps on the earth." 27 So God created man in His own image; in the image of God He created him; male and female He created them. 28 Then God blessed them, and God said to them, "Be fruitful and multiply; fill the earth and subdue it; have dominion over the fish of the sea, over the birds of the air, and over every living thing that moves on the earth."

Genesis 1:26-28 NKJV

When God made man, He made man in His image; God made His children to be like Him. He gave man dominion over the earth and it was man's responsibility to govern the earth. Unfortunately, when Adam decided to disobey God's command, Adam gave his authority away to Satan.

Thankfully, God already had a plan in place; the plan's name was Jesus! Jesus was the second Adam and Jesus came to restore not only our position of righteousness with God, but also to restore our authority on the earth. Through Jesus death, burial and resurrection, Jesus took back the keys of death, Hell and the grave.

19 and what is the exceeding greatness of His power toward us who believe, according to the working of His mighty power 20 which He worked in Christ when He raised Him from the dead and seated Him at His right hand in the heavenly places, 21 far above all principality and power and might and dominion, and every name that is named, not only in this age but also in that which is to come. 22 And He put all things under His feet, and gave Him to be head over all things to the church, 23 which is His body, the fullness of Him who fills all in all.

Ephesians 1:19-23 NKJV

God raised up Jesus and seated Him at His right hand in Heaven. Jesus was given the highest position of authority and was given dominion over everything. Notice the Bible says that everything was put under His feet! I want you to notice even more so that we are the body of Christ; therefore, no matter what your position is within the Body of Christ, you share in Jesus authority too! This is why Jesus went on to declare not only what He had received, but also what He was giving to us in the Great Commission.

18 Jesus came and told his disciples, "I have been given all authority in heaven and on earth. 19 Therefore, go and make disciples of all the nations, baptizing them in the name of the Father and the Son and the Holy Spirit.

Matthew 28:18-19 NLT

Jesus got our authority back and because we are united to Him, the same authority Jesus had, He conferred it to us. When God raised up Jesus from the dead, He raised us up from the dead also. We shared not only in His death and resurrection, but also in His seating in Heaven at God's right hand.

4 But God, who is rich in mercy, because of His great love with which He loved us, 5 even when we were dead in trespasses, made us alive together with Christ (by grace you have been saved), 6 and raised us up together, and made us sit together in the heavenly places in Christ Jesus.

Ephesians 2:4-6 NKJV

This is why we don't have to worry about natural disasters, storms, plagues or even financial depressions. Satan is under Jesus feet and is therefore under our feet; as a result, anything that is of Satan is under our feet too.

Let's take a look at the authority Jesus operated with in the earth. One of my favorites is Jesus calming the storm.

23 Now when He got into a boat, His disciples followed Him. 24 And suddenly a great tempest arose on the sea, so that the boat was covered with the waves. But He was asleep. 25 Then His disciples came to Him and awoke Him, saying, "Lord, save us! We are perishing!" 26 But He said to them, "Why are you fearful, O you of little faith?" Then He arose and rebuked the winds and the sea, and there was a great calm. 27 So the men marveled, saying, "Who can this be, that even the

winds and the sea obey Him?"

Matthew 8:23-27 NKJV

The authority Jesus operated in was so powerful that people noticed it; they realized Jesus was different. Not only did Jesus exercise His authority over storms, He also readily exercised His authority over sickness and disease. One story that has always stood out to me regarding Jesus authority is that of the Roman centurion.

5 When Jesus returned to Capernaum, a Roman officer came and pleaded with him, 6 "Lord, my young servant lies in bed, paralyzed and in terrible pain." 7 Jesus said, "I will come and heal him." 8 But the officer said, "Lord, I am not worthy to have you come into my home. Just say the word from where you are, and my servant will be healed. 9 I know this because I am under the authority of my superior officers, and I have authority over my soldiers. I only need to say, 'Go,' and they go, or 'Come,' and they come. And if I say to my slaves, 'Do this,' they do it." 10 When Jesus heard this, he was amazed. Turning to those who were following him, he said, "I tell you the truth, I haven't seen faith like this in all Israel! 11 And I tell you this, that many Gentiles will come from all over the world—from

east and west—and sit down with Abraham, Isaac, and Jacob at the feast in the Kingdom of Heaven. 12 But many Israelites—those for whom the Kingdom was prepared—will be thrown into outer darkness, where there will be weeping and gnashing of teeth." 13 Then Jesus said to the Roman officer, "Go back home. Because you believed, it has happened." And the young servant was healed that same hour.

Matthew 8:5-13 NLT

All Jesus had to do was speak the Word. There was no pomp and circumstance about it; it was simply Jesus exercising His God given authority. I want you to notice not only the authority Jesus operated in, but also the fact He didn't have to try and work something up. His authority was a natural part of Him because Jesus knew who He was and who He represented.

26 For as the Father has life in Himself, so He has granted the Son to have life in Himself, 27 and has given Him authority to execute judgment also, because He is the Son of Man.

John 5:26-27 NKJV

49 For I have not spoken on My own authority; but

the Father who sent Me gave Me a command, what I
should say and what I should speak.

John 12:49 NKJV

10 Do you not believe that I am in the Father, and the
Father in Me? The words that I speak to you I do not
speak on My own authority; but the Father who dwells
in Me does the works.

John 14:10 NKJV

Jesus wasn't following a faith formula; Jesus was so
consumed with His union with God that His awareness
of God working through Him dominated Jesus life and
ministry. The authority of Jesus and the faith in that
authority stemmed from the supernatural relationship
Jesus had with God. So when negative situations arose,
Jesus didn't have to pull out a manual or start reciting
confessions. Jesus didn't try to do; He naturally responded
exactly like God would with supernatural results.

Authority Over Demons

I've seen people trying to cast out demons and you would
have thought it was a circus act. One time I had a minister
tell me he would stretch his arms and legs to prepare

himself to go to battle with the devil when it was time to cast one out. He told me there had been several times that he and others had wrestled with demon possessed people for hours trying to get a demon out. The sad part was he thought he was really being spiritual; unfortunately, he was simply revealing his lack of understanding of his authority.

Jesus didn't wrestle and have tag team matches trying to get a devil out of someone. Jesus was a man operating under God's authority on the earth; He simply spoke the word of God and the demons had to obey. Casting out a devil is as easy as flicking a fly!

28 When Jesus arrived on the other side of the lake, in the region of the Gadarenes, two men who were possessed by demons met him. They lived in a cemetery and were so violent that no one could go through that area. 29 They began screaming at him, "Why are you interfering with us, Son of God? Have you come here to torture us before God's appointed time?" 30 There happened to be a large herd of pigs feeding in the distance. 31 So the demons begged, "If you cast us out, send us into that herd of pigs." 32 "All right, go!" Jesus commanded them. So the demons came out of the men and entered the pigs, and the

whole herd plunged down the steep hillside into the lake and drowned in the water. 33 The herdsmen fled to the nearby town, telling everyone what happened to the demon-possessed men. 34 Then the entire town came out to meet Jesus, but they begged him to go away and leave them alone.

Matthew 8:28-34 NLT

I remember one time there was a lady who came to our church in Texas. She had visited twice on a Wednesday night and each time, it was obvious that something wasn't necessarily right with her. I really am not concerned with what people wear to church, but in her situation, she was pretty bad off. During one of the services, an usher had to offer her a blanket to cover up her backside because half of her rear end was hanging out of her pants! Her hair was a mess and she simply looked like she hadn't showered in quite a while.

Now, even though I knew something wasn't right with her, I didn't just go up to her and start demanding a devil to come out. I wasn't for sure what the problem was and you telling someone they have a demon when you aren't sure just isn't smart. I've seen too many people that assumed every problem was demonic possession and those people usually ended up hurting more people than they helped.

Well, several weeks later we were conducting a healing crusade and this lady was in attendance. At the end, she came up to the front with several others for healing. When I put my hand on her shoulder, I knew beyond a shadow of a doubt there was demonic involvement. Now I wasn't seeking after a gift of the Spirit, but again, I know the Holy Spirit knows what I need when I need it, so I was just looking to Him. I immediately commanded that foul spirit to come out of her.

At that point, her face began to change somewhat and she began to back up a little bit and walk away; well, I followed her telling that demon he had to come out. After a few minutes, she sat down and it was obvious something happened because her whole countenance changed for the better.

After that service, we didn't see her for several months. One Sunday morning, a nicely dressed woman and her boyfriend walked passed me in the foyer. I greeted them and told them I was glad to have them visiting the church that day. She looked at me and said, "Pastor Chad, you don't recognize me do you?" Honestly, I didn't; I wasn't aware this was the same woman we had cast the demon out of months before. She didn't even look like the same person! She was dressed well, her hair and makeup was done, she had a nice new boyfriend and a new job!

Your Authority Doesn't Need Additives

The reason I'm telling you this story is because I want you to see that I didn't have to put on some show to use my authority as a believer. I didn't have to get a special song going and I didn't put on my Hulk Hogan gear to wrestle with some stupid devil. When you know your authority in Christ, you don't have to add anything natural with it. The authority of Christ doesn't need fleshy additives!

The same authority Jesus has, you and I have and we are expected to use it to the fullest. We don't have to try and work something up to use it and we certainly don't have to feel a certain way. Some days you may feel like the weakest person on the planet, but remember, it's not about how you feel; it's about what you know.

We can see this in Jesus dealing with the disciples. In the beginning of Jesus ministry, He called the twelve disciples together and gave them authority over every sickness, disease and devil and then told them to use it.

> **1 One day Jesus called together his twelve disciples and gave them power and authority to cast out all demons and to heal all diseases. 2 Then he sent them out to tell everyone about the Kingdom of God and to heal the sick. 3 "Take nothing for your journey," he instructed them. "Don't take a walking stick, a traveler's bag, food, money, or even a change of clothes. 4 Wherever you go, stay in the same house until you leave town. 5 And if a town refuses to welcome you, shake its dust from your feet as you leave to show that you have abandoned those people to their fate." 6 So they began their circuit of the villages, preaching the Good News and healing the sick.**
>
> **Luke 9:1-6 NLT**

Look at Jesus instructions. Did you notice instructions on how to get the supernatural to work? No, instead, Jesus instructions are regarding their belongings and how to respond to people. In regards to the supernatural, Jesus instructions were simple: "I give you authority to cast out devils and heal the sick. Now get to it boys!" Jesus didn't mention anything about a special oil, shawl, horn, music, dance, feeling, or any of the other natural things we use to try and get the power of God to show up.

When you have to try and work something up to get the supernatural to show up, you need to stop what you are doing, back up and get back under God's grace. Someone that has authority in a situation doesn't need "extra" stuff to make their authority work.

It's interesting to look at how Jesus used His authority versus the way most of us use our authority. When Jesus demanded something to obey, His commands were short and to the point. He would say things like, "Peace be still," "Go your way," or "Come forth!" One of the longest commands you will find in the Gospels is when Jesus dealt with the demon possessed boy.

> **25 When Jesus saw that the crowd of onlookers was growing, he rebuked the evil spirit. "Listen, you spirit that makes this boy unable to hear and speak," he said. "I command you to come out of this child and never enter him again!"**
>
> **Mark 9:25 NLT**

Jesus commands had power and were backed by His authority. He knew His authority, so He didn't beat around the bush. Jesus spoke directly and concisely. We on the other hand usually preach a sermon when we are taking authority over a situation.

Seriously, think about it. Think about the last time you saw someone being ministered to for healing. Was it a simple command or a mini sermon?

When my dog is getting in the trash, I yell out, "Rocky, get out of the trash!" I don't calmly and politely say, "Now Rocky, I want you to know that I have authority over you. You know you aren't supposed to be in the trash and I'm not going to put up with it anymore. I'm telling you right now to get out of the trash and stay out of the trash. The Bible says…"

I don't debate with sin, I don't lecture sickness and I don't have a conversation with tornados. If it isn't supposed to be there and I have authority over it, it won't have to listen long because I won't be talking long.

Have Faith In Your Authority

Could it be the reason our commands of authority are so long is because we don't have much faith in them? For whatever reason, we think a prayer or command has to be long to be powerful and that just isn't the case.

I remember a situation two years ago when a woman came up at the end of the service for healing. She had some severe lower back pain and wanted prayer. I simply spoke to her back and said, "In the Name of Jesus, pain be gone." She looked at me and said, "That's it?" I laughed and asked what she was expecting. She said, "I just thought you would pray longer." I responded by saying, "That's all I needed to say. Go ahead and bend over and you will see that all the pain is gone." She bent over, touched her toes and was instantly healed.

I can personally attest to being long winded in my commands of authority years ago, but one day the Holy Spirit got my attention when I was studying and began to talk to me about it. I started looking at how Jesus used His authority and how I used mine. I started realizing I didn't have as much confidence in it as Jesus did; otherwise, I wouldn't have felt the need to give it a boost.

Notice the word *felt*. I found out I had more faith in my long windedness than my authority; I basically would speak until I felt I had done something. I had forgotten what Jesus said about our prayers and commands until the

Holy Spirit reminded me.

> 7 **"When you pray, don't babble on and on as people of other religions do. They think their prayers are answered merely by repeating their words again and again.**
>
> **Matthew 6:7 NLT**

It may not seem like a big deal, but friend, I want results just like Jesus. In the beginning, it may mean changing big things, but as you go on, you'll find small, but necessary changes that will be required for increased results. When I made this change, I started experiencing more results.

Since I began in ministry, I have always seen very good results in the area of healing. I have experienced firsthand the blind see and deaf hear, tumors dissolve, legs grow…all sorts of wonderful things. Over the years of my yielding and changing, I have progressively seen greater results in greater ways. Two years ago, things really began to change in my ministry. I have always laid hands on people, but I started doing more speaking and started experiencing tremendous results.

The Girl With The Dislocated Shoulder

I'll never forget a youth conference I preached at in Spokane, Washington. There was a young girl who had injured her shoulder as a result of swimming. She was a competitive swimmer and due to the constant rotation of her arm, she had injured the ligaments in her right shoulder. Because of the ligament injury, it would sometimes cause her shoulder to pop out of socket; during the conference, it had popped out.

During one of the evening services, this girl came to the front along with a number of other students who were in need of healing. She was the very first one and I distinctly remember seeing her right arm hanging much lower than her left. She told me about her swimming injury and about her shoulder popping out. Usually, I would have the person show me and the crowd what they could currently do in their situation; then, after we minister to them, everyone can see the change. This situation was a little different in that she couldn't move it and it was obvious to the eye something was wrong.

I asked her if she was ready to be healed and she nodded her head. I looked at her right shoulder and said, "In the

Name of Jesus, be made whole." Immediately, I watched her right arm lift up and pop back into place. She lifted her right arm up and began to rotate it all around. God had restored full rotation to her shoulder!

I would be lying if I said I felt something before, during or after I spoke. I didn't get the Holy Ghost shakes and didn't try to make her fall either. I wasn't interested in her falling down under the power; I was interested in her being healed by the power.

Falling Under The Power

Let's talk about falling under the power for a moment. I'm not negating the reality of it. I've had people lay hands on me, speak over me and I have legitimately been under the power of God to such a degree, my physical body couldn't take it and I fell to the ground in a heap. There were also times when I was a teenager (and didn't know any better) that a preacher prayed for me, I looked backwards for the usher and then I fell back into their secure arms.

The reason I did that as a youngster was because it was expected. Falling out was expected by the minister and expected by the receiver. As a kid, I just did what I saw other people do: make sure you had a catcher before you "experienced" God.

I've seen a lot of ministers that focus more on people falling out than getting healed. You can tell because they keep praying and telling the person to receive until the person does fall out. (Sometimes I think people fall out just so the minister will stop!) Let me clue you in on something: someone falling out isn't the proof they received their healing. I've been pushed – literally – on a number of occasions by ministers and that didn't do anything for me.

If people fall, fine; it doesn't make me any difference. My focus is getting them to receive the power of God. I would much rather them sit in a chair and focus on the life of God being imparted into them than falling out on the floor. This may go cross grain against some people's theology, but I don't really care; I want results like Jesus.

Just as a side note, show me one person that Jesus ministered healing to that fell out under the power – you won't find even one. Again, am I saying that falling under the power isn't real? By all means no. In some situations it is real and I have experienced it; however, I do believe we again have focused on something natural to get the supernatural to happen.

When people have learned by either observation or experience to check for an usher behind them before they receive the power, something is wrong. When the minister has to rely on someone falling out to know they received, something is wrong. Do you want to know a good way to find out if they received the healing power? If they were healed!

We need to stop acting carnal and grow up in spiritual things. When you know who you are in Christ and you know what you possess in Christ, you won't rely on natural things to produce a supernatural result. If spectacular things happen, great - just don't let them be your focus.

The Name Of Jesus

If we will simply understand the authority we have in the Name of Jesus, I mean really understand it, it would revolutionize Christianity. In the Name of Jesus carries the power, the authority and the weight of Jesus Himself. Let me give you one more example of someone using their authority in Christ and getting results.

1 Peter and John went to the Temple one afternoon to take part in the three o'clock prayer service. 2 As they approached the Temple, a man lame from birth was being carried in. Each day he was put beside the Temple gate, the one called the Beautiful Gate, so he could beg from the people going into the Temple. 3 When he saw Peter and John about to enter, he asked them for some money. 4 Peter and John looked at him intently, and Peter said, "Look at us!" 5 The lame man looked at them eagerly, expecting some money. 6 But Peter said, "I don't have any silver or gold for you. But I'll give you what I have. In the name of Jesus Christ the Nazarene, get up and walk!" 7 Then Peter took the lame man by the right hand and helped him up. And as he did, the man's feet and ankles were instantly healed and strengthened. 8 He jumped up, stood on his feet, and began to walk! Then, walking, leaping, and praising God, he went into the Temple with them.

Acts 3:1-8 NLT

Peter used his authority in Christ like a boss! He made one short statement backed by the Name of Jesus: "In the Name of Jesus Christ the Nazarene, get up and walk!" No mini sermon. No quoting of the top ten healing scriptures. Nothing spectacular and nothing show worthy; just a command backed by Heaven.

For Peter, commanding the man to be healed was no different than Jesus Himself doing it. Peter didn't have to put on a show. Peter didn't have to talk a long time to convince himself, the devil, the man, and everyone else that he meant business. Peter just did what he saw Jesus do and expected results. He had seen Jesus use the authority that God had given Him to judge sickness and disease to be wrong on the earth.

The authority of Jesus invested in us allows us to release the life of God on this earth just like Jesus did. This authority is part of our supernatural equipment to live a supernatural life on a natural planet; therefore, allowing us to get results just like it was Jesus doing it Himself.

Chapter 15
Supernatural Love

5 Now hope does not disappoint, because the love of God has been poured out in our hearts by the Holy Spirit who was given to us.

Romans 5:5 NKJV

The love of God is powerful and that love was poured out in our spirit in abundance. The love of God allows us to overcome anything that comes our way. It's vitally important we understand this because many times it is easy to be moved by our feelings. If we don't allow the love of God to flow, it will be impossible to fulfill what God has called us to do. You can't be naturally supernatural without the love of God.

When we meditate on our union with Christ and allow

everything that flows from the Vine to flow into us, the love of God will flow out of you like a mighty rushing river. You will love the unlovable and be absolutely unstoppable. You will find that the love of God will compel you to move beyond your emotions, beyond your mind and into an arena where the supernatural becomes very natural.

If we look at the ministry of Jesus, you see a Man overflowing with the love of God for humanity and it was this love that resulted in many, many miracles.

> **14 And when Jesus went out He saw a great multitude; and He was moved with compassion for them, and healed their sick.**
>
> **Matthew 14:14 NKJV**

Faith doesn't stem from a formula; faith stems from a union with Almighty God. Because we share God's nature, His love will move you with compassion to bring healing to the world. It's why I love the healing ministry so very much. When I see people that are crippled, diseased and given no hope, there is a love that rises up from my spirit yearning to see those people healed.

> **40 Now a leper came to Him, imploring Him, kneeling down to Him and saying to Him, "If You are willing,**

You can make me clean." 41 Then Jesus, moved with compassion, stretched out His hand and touched him, and said to him, "I am willing; be cleansed." 42 As soon as He had spoken, immediately the leprosy left him, and he was cleansed.

Mark 1:40-42 NKJV

I love this passage of Scripture. Here we see not only Jesus love for people and His desire to see people healed, we also see that the love of God will move you past the realities of this world. The leper was not questioning Jesus power, but His willingness. To answer the leper's question, Jesus first responds with an act of love; He reached out and touched the leper.

There is no telling how long it had been since the leper had actually experienced the touch of another human being because lepers were outcasts. The love of Jesus was so powerful that it moved Him to do what other people wouldn't do; Jesus touched the leper. The love of Jesus not only moved Him to touch the leper, but the love of Jesus released the life of God into the man's body.

Jesus wasn't focused on His authority. Jesus wasn't focused on a gift of the Spirit. Jesus wasn't focused on a feeling. Jesus was simply focused on a man being set free. As soon as Jesus spoke, the leprosy left.

The Boy With Hodgkin's Disease

There is one particular healing that took place in our ministry I will never forget; it impacted me so greatly and helped me to understand the compassion of Jesus. It was a Sunday morning in October of 2006. We were at the close of the service when we began to pray for the sick and an older woman came to the front with her four year old grandson. When I asked what was wrong, she told me he had three tumors on top of his head and had recently been diagnosed with Hodgkin's disease.

I put my right hand on the top of his head and felt the tumors; there was one about the size of a quarter and two others the size of a pea. I picked him up and we cursed that cancer; then, I told the congregation to join with me in thanking God for the miracle taking place in that sweet little boy's body.

As I was holding the boy, I still had my right hand on his head. I held him that way for around ten minutes as we just continued to praise God. During that time, a love

I had never really experienced before just began to pour through me and I began to weep profusely. Suddenly, I felt the tumors begin to dissolve under my hand. It was like someone put a pin in a balloon and the air was slowly coming out of them. I called the grandmother over and said, "Grandma, you've got to feel this!" She came running over and began to run her hand over his head. She exclaimed, "The two small ones are gone and the big one is shrinking!" Over the next few minutes, the tumor that started out the size of a quarter was down to about the size of a pea while the other two completely dissolved away.

The little boy had a doctor's appointment two days later for a checkup and new scans. The grandmother called me a few days later and she was ecstatic. She told me, "Pastor Chad, the next day, the last remaining tumor went completely away. We just received the results of the new scans and the doctor reported that there are no more signs of Hodgkin's disease!"

It was in that moment I got a glimpse of the power of God's love. Not only is it important for us to understand this supernatural love, it's important that we help others understand God's love for them.

The Man Who Fell Through A Roof

On Easter Sunday in 2010, we were finishing up with the worship part of the service when Lacy walked up to the platform and stopped everything. She said, "I just talked to a husband and wife in the foyer who told me the only reason they came to church this morning was to get healed. This man broke his back several years ago and even with surgery, it never fully healed." She then looked at me and said, "So, Pastor is going to come up here and minister to him."

I kind of imagined myself as Jesus at the wedding when they ran out of wine and Mary said, "Whatever Jesus says to do, do it." Lacy sort of forced a miracle on me! It is funny looking back, but at the moment, I wasn't in the "healing mood." I had been off in my own little world just worshipping God and thinking about my message for that morning.

Well, I put my faith face on and acted like I knew what I was doing! The man was a rather large man and he obviously was in a great deal of pain, so one of the ushers got him a chair to sit in. I asked him what happened and he explained that he used to be a roofer, but five years ago, he fell through a soft spot on a roof and broke his back. As a result of the break, the surgeon had to fuse several of the bones, but even with the surgery, it never fully healed and he had continued to be in severe pain.

Now again, when I say I wasn't in the healing mood, I mean I wasn't feeling anything. So, I knew what I needed to do. I opened my mouth and said, "Who here has never seen someone get instantly healed?" In the very back row, there were four young ladies that raised their hands. I said, "You ladies come up here and sit on the front row and watch what's going to happen."

You see, I had to get past my feelings and one of the best ways I knew how to do that was to get past myself and put the pressure on the Holy Spirit. Smith Wigglesworth once said, "If the Spirit isn't moving, I make Him move." I knew exactly what Smith was talking about because that's what I was doing this particular morning!

So I looked at the man and said, "I want you to stand up." Well, he was so large and in so much pain, it took myself and two of the ushers to help him stand up. I then put my hands on his back, commanded his back to be healed and then told the man to bend over. He bent over a little bit but I could tell nothing had really happened. He was in excruciating pain and tears were running down his eyes – and they weren't tears of joy either! So, I had him sit back down.

Now I'll admit, I was a little perplexed. I spoke faith words and meant what I said. I put God on the spot by having those four women come up to watch a miracle, but nothing happened. Well, this is where you find out if you are a man or a boy! I could have sent him back to his chair and encouraged him to "just keep believing brother" like so many do or I could act like Jesus and get this man healed. Well, because I wanted to see this man healed and I wanted to save my pride, I determined to press forward; so, I told everyone to start praying in the Spirit.

Knowing God's love will cause the supernatural to flow.

Now while everyone was praying, I was saying under my breath, "Alright God, what's the deal?" "How do I get out of this?" Suddenly, I thought about a song called *How He Loves* by the David Crowder Band. So, I told our music team to start playing it. (Sometimes, being led by the Spirit is one baby step at a time!) I didn't know what else to do, so we just sang *How He Loves* for a few minutes. As we were singing, I got a word of knowledge about the man's parents in that his parents never truly treated him with love and as a result, he had assumed it was the same way with God. When I relayed this information to him, he told me I was right; he didn't think God really loved him. His ignorance of God's love for him was hindering him from receiving.

So, I took a few moments and talked to him about the love of God as tears began to flow down his face again. I then told everyone to begin singing the song again and so we all began to sing, "He loves us! Oh how He loves us! Oh how He loves us; how He loves us so!" I stood beside the man with my left hand on his shoulder as we simply sung about the love of God when suddenly, the man started getting up. With no help, he stood straight up, bent over and touched his toes. The man was instantly healed and it was all because of a revelation of God's love.

Get Rid Of Offense

Friend, God's love is powerful. It will not only cause healing to flow, it will also cause forgiveness to flow. If you want to live a supernatural life, you must learn how to flow in supernatural forgiveness. I'm talking about allowing the love of God to flow through you so powerfully that you allow that love to cover a multitude of sins and you refuse to carry any offense that may have come your way. Look at what Jesus said in Mark 11.

22 So Jesus answered and said to them, "Have faith in God. 23 For assuredly, I say to you, whoever says to this mountain, 'Be removed and be cast into the sea,' and does not doubt in his heart, but believes that those things he says will be done, he will have whatever he says. 24 Therefore I say to you, whatever things you ask when you pray, believe that you receive them, and you will have them. 25 "And whenever you stand praying, if you have anything against anyone, forgive him, that your Father in heaven may also forgive you your trespasses.

Mark 11:22-25 NKJV

This is a passage about faith, but it's also a passage about love. Notice the connection between faith and love. You can't live a supernatural life without walking in supernatural love. There is nothing that will stop the supernatural power of God in your life faster than offense which really has its root in stinking, nasty, rotten pride.

It's one of the reasons why Jesus, in the midst of being nailed to the cross and enduring horrific pain, was able to not only forgive those before Him, but also minister to the thief beside Him. Jesus had every reason to be offended because He had done nothing wrong; however, He refused to allow the love of God to be shut off so the supernatural could still flow. I guarantee Jesus wasn't feeling too spiritual at that moment, but being spiritual isn't about a feeling. When you make a decision to walk in your union with God, His love will flow through you.

Chapter 16
Embrace His Grace

17 For the sin of this one man, Adam, caused death to rule over many. But even greater is God's wonderful grace and his gift of righteousness, for all who receive it will live in triumph over sin and death through this one man, Jesus Christ.

Romans 5:17 NLT

Once we begin to understand the supernatural people that we are and the supernatural equipment that we have, we must walk in it. God wants us to know what we have and it is why repeatedly, the apostle Paul continued to tell us what we have – over and over and over.

In Romans 5:17, we get a great summary statement of

God's intention for us; God wants us to triumph in life, but the triumph can only come when we live through Christ. We have a lot of well-meaning Christians who have right intentions and come off sounding spiritual, but are bound with religion and therefore are producing little results in the supernatural realm. The reason is because of two words: grace and righteousness.

Let's define and expound on these two words for a moment. The grace of God could simply be defined as what God did for you independent of you; it was God's grace that provides access to the supernatural life.

A lot of us are trying to get spiritual enough to do something for God. We are making our confessions, reading our chapters, blowing shofars, shouting loud, crying hard and everything else physically we can think of as to how to get God's power to show up. It's why so many are endeavoring to work a formula or principles to experience the power of God when it has nothing to do with a formula. It has everything to do with His grace that not only opened the door, but put us in the position to experience and manifest the supernatural.

Righteousness goes right along with God's grace.

Righteousness puts us in the position to experience what grace provided. We could also say it like this: righteousness is the position to use God's equipment (grace).

The understanding of God's grace has really gone by the wayside for a lot of faith people. Over the years, many who know the principles of faith have really turned them into works of faith and as a result, nullified the grace of God. Take a look at what God's grace did for us.

4 But God is so rich in mercy, and he loved us so much, 5 that even though we were dead because of our sins, he gave us life when he raised Christ from the dead. (It is only by God's grace that you have been saved!) 6 For he raised us from the dead along with Christ and seated us with him in the heavenly realms because we are united with Christ Jesus.

Ephesians 2:4-6 NLT

How was salvation provided? Was it because of our great faith? Was it because of our confessions or Bible reading? No. Salvation was provided because of God's grace. It was our faith in His grace that saved us; it was God's grace that provided a union with Christ. It was God's grace that infused us with dead raising Holy Spirit power. It was God's grace that provided it all – independent of us. There were no formulas, steps, principles or any other natural works we could do that could get us what grace provided. Our only responsibility was to simply put our faith in His grace. Once we believed what He did, every spiritual blessing in Heavenly places in Christ became ours.

As soon as we accepted God's grace, before we ever had one opportunity to lift a finger and prove ourselves, God sat us down in Christ at the highest place of authority. The first thing God did with you once you were saved was to make you rest! Why? It was not because of what we had done; it was because we were now united with Christ.

I see so many Christians frustrated because they are working so hard without any results. They know the Scriptures, but they don't know their union. Jesus is the Vine and we are the branches. The vine was created to do all the work, not the branches. We aren't supposed to be working to get the supernatural to work in our lives; because of our union with Christ, it should simply now be a natural outflow of who we are.

1 God's promise of entering his rest still stands, so we ought to tremble with fear that some of you might fail

to experience it. 2 For this good news—that God has prepared this rest—has been announced to us just as it was to them. But it did them no good because they didn't share the faith of those who listened to God. 3 For only we who believe can enter his rest. As for the others, God said, "In my anger I took an oath: 'They will never enter my place of rest,'" even though this rest has been ready since he made the world. 4 We know it is ready because of the place in the Scriptures where it mentions the seventh day: "On the seventh day God rested from all his work."

Hebrews 4:1-4 NLT

The Christian life, the supernatural life, is a life of rest and God gave Himself as an example. Why did God rest? God rested because everything man would need was already provided. When God was creating the world, He made sure mankind had water, shelter, food, gold and everything else man would need to triumph in life.

God was so interested in man being successful and fulfilling the plan of God that God provided everything else first and then made Adam. Did you ever notice God's steps of creation? He didn't make Adam on the first day; God made Adam on the last day. If God would have made

Adam on the first day, Adam would have been treading water for two days! God had enough forethought to provide all the equipment Adam would need before He put Adam into existence.

This is exactly what God did for us. Through Jesus, God provided everything we would ever need to triumph in life. God's grace provided it all!

3 All praise to God, the Father of our Lord Jesus Christ, who has blessed us with every spiritual blessing in the heavenly realms because we are united with Christ.
Ephesians 1:3 NLT

It's Time To Rest

We've been given everything we need by God's grace; this is why we shouldn't be relying on natural works to either get something to happen or try to bend God's arm to give us what He already gave us. Isn't it amazing God actually believed He finished everything for you and I?

Listening to most Christians, you would think God still is holding out on finishing the job for us – but not God!

God so believed the work was finished in Christ that He rested and even Jesus rested. So if God is resting and Jesus is resting in the finished work, why aren't you and I?

6 Since therefore it remains that some must enter it, and those to whom it was first preached did not enter because of disobedience, 7 again He designates a certain day, saying in David, "Today," after such a long time, as it has been said: "Today, if you will hear His voice, Do not harden your hearts." 8 For if Joshua had given them rest, then He would not afterward have spoken of another day. 9 There remains therefore a rest for the people of God. 10 For he who has entered His rest has himself also ceased from his works as God did from His. 11 Let us therefore be diligent to enter that rest, lest anyone fall according to the same example of disobedience.

Hebrews 4:6-11 NLT

The Israelites didn't enter into God's promise because they looked to themselves; they were self-reliant. Unfortunately, this is exactly what is going on within Christianity right now. We've stepped outside the grace of God and have begun relying on our works to get the supernatural to manifest in our lives.

The Ultimate Deception

It's human nature to look to ourselves and why the bestselling topics of books right now are self-help – even in the Christian sections! Satan has been telling a lie and Christians keep believing it. We don't think we have enough of what we need to get the job done. It's been Satan's tactic since the beginning of time.

1 The serpent was the shrewdest of all the wild animals the Lord God had made. One day he asked the woman, "Did God really say you must not eat the fruit from any of the trees in the garden?" 2 "Of course we may eat fruit from the trees in the garden," the woman replied. 3 "It's only the fruit from the tree in the middle of the garden that we are not allowed to eat. God said, 'You must not eat it or even touch it; if you do, you will die.'" 4 "You won't die!" the serpent replied to the woman. 5 "God knows that your eyes will be opened as soon as you eat it, and you will be like God, knowing both good and evil." 6 The woman was convinced. She saw that the tree was beautiful and its fruit looked delicious, and she wanted the wisdom it would give her. So she took some of the fruit and ate it. Then she gave some to her husband, who was with

her, and he ate it, too. 7 At that moment their eyes were opened, and they suddenly felt shame at their nakedness. So they sewed fig leaves together to cover themselves.

Genesis 3:1-7 NLT

Satan told Eve that she wasn't like God, but if she would do something, she could become like God. It was the ultimate deception. Do you know why? God's grace had already given Eve everything she would ever need; God's grace had already made Eve like God, but she didn't know it. Because Eve did not know, then she tried to rely on her works, on her smarts, on her creativity and on a natural work to make herself supernatural. On Satan's part, it was genius. Eve didn't know her union with God so Satan got her to work for what she already had and it led to her losing it.

It's time that we realize who we are, what we have and rest in that knowledge. Instead of putting your faith in your works, put your faith in what Jesus already has done; when you do, that is when you begin to experience supernatural results in a very natural way.

Chapter 17
We Win Over Sin

5 For if we have been united together in the likeness of His death, certainly we also shall be in the likeness of His resurrection, 6 knowing this, that our old man was crucified with Him, that the body of sin might be done away with, that we should no longer be slaves of sin. 7 For he who has died has been freed from sin.

Romans 6:5-7 NKJV

As a spirit being united with Christ, one thing we shouldn't be struggling with is sin; unfortunately, way too many of us are battling to overcome sin. Working and battling to win isn't the way Jesus set this thing up! The Gospel is the good news; it's the almost too good to be true news! It's the good news that you don't have to work to win because Jesus already won for you. I don't battle; I just win!

When we become one with Christ, the power sin had over us was eradicated. We went from being sin's slave to being sin's master. Romans 6:7 tells us that because the old us died with Christ, we have been freed from sin. Well, if we have been freed from sin, then how come so many of us are struggling to get free? It is because we haven't understood our union with Christ.

The supernatural power of God will flow from Jesus out of your spirit into your soul and body to free you from any bad habit, any addiction and any sin that is weighing you down. Jesus didn't die so you could try and free yourself; Jesus died so He could free you.

If you are trying to free yourself, you have stepped outside of the grace of God and your union with Christ. You can work the twelve steps or you can simply rest in what Jesus already did for you. Jesus set you free!

Do Some Considering

8 Now if we died with Christ, we believe that we shall also live with Him, 9 knowing that Christ, having been raised from the dead, dies no more. Death no

longer has dominion over Him. 10 For the death that He died, He died to sin once for all; but the life that He lives, He lives to God. 11 Likewise you also, reckon yourselves to be dead indeed to sin, but alive to God in Christ Jesus our Lord.

Romans 8:8-11 NKJV

Notice Romans 8:11 says, "Likewise you also, reckon…" By saying "likewise," God is telling us we need to do something just like Jesus did. What did Jesus do? Jesus reckoned Himself dead to sin, but alive to God.

What does the word *reckon* mean? *Reckon* means "to consider or believe that something is true." Well, do you have to consider something to be true that is obviously true? Certainly not. I don't look in the mirror each day and have to consider the truth that I am Chad Gonzales! It is very apparent that I am Chad, not my wife Lacy!

So we see here that just like Jesus, you and I will have to do some considering of truths in order to experience the reality of those truths. What it really comes down to is renewing our mind to the realities of our redemption and righteousness.

So if you are a believer and you are still struggling in an

area, what do you need to do? The first step is you need to consider yourself dead to sin. You need to know sin no longer can dominate you. *The only thing you need to work on is not getting free, but knowing you are free!*

The battle is not getting free from sin; the battle is changing your thinking to knowing sin no longer has authority and power over you. When you make that change, the supernatural power of God naturally will start flowing through you and setting you free quicker than you ever could have done on your own.

The problem is we have accepted natural facts that according to psychology, it takes twenty one days to change a habit. Well, if you don't have Jesus, that may be so, but if you are unified with Christ and His life flows through you, that bad habit can disappear in the blink of an eye! Jesus didn't die so you could be free in twenty one days! Jesus

Jesus doesn't need 21 days to set you free!

died and rose back up so you could be free when you said, "Jesus be the Lord and Savior of my life!"

The second step is to consider yourself alive to God in Christ! You need to know you are one with Jesus and as a result, you walk in His freedom, His authority and His righteousness.

18 And having been set free from sin, you became slaves of righteousness. 19 I speak in human terms because of the weakness of your flesh. For just as you presented your members as slaves of uncleanness, and of lawlessness leading to more lawlessness, so now present your members as slaves of righteousness for holiness. 20 For when you were slaves of sin, you were free in regard to righteousness. 21 What fruit did you have then in the things of which you are now ashamed? For the end of those things is death. 22 But now having been set free from sin, and having become slaves of God, you have your fruit to holiness, and the end, everlasting life.

Romans 6:18-22 NKJV

When you know who you are in Christ and what has been done for you, you can present yourself to God, the world and Satan as a master over sin and a slave unto righteousness. Now instead of sin naturally flowing out of you, righteousness naturally flows out of you. Your union with Christ gave you God's righteousness and as a natural by-product of having God's nature within you, the fruits of righteousness and holiness will automatically be produced.

Never forget that Jesus is the Vine and you are the branch. The vine is responsible for getting all the necessary stuff to the branch for fruit to be produced. It's not the branches responsibility to produce the fruit; it's the vine's responsibility to produce fruit. The only responsibility the branch has is to stay connected to the vine. What is the result? Fruit is naturally produced.

Jesus never meant for you to go to battle and try to conquer; if that was the case, Jesus didn't do a good enough job with redemption! However, we know that isn't the case; God's plan of redemption was flawless!

37 Yet in all these things we are more than conquerors through Him who loved us.

Romans 8:37 NKJV

57 But thanks be to God, who gives us the victory through our Lord Jesus Christ.

1 Corinthians 15:57 NKJV

14 Now thanks be to God who always leads us in triumph in Christ, and through us diffuses the

fragrance of His knowledge in every place.

2 Corinthians 2:14 NKJV

Look at these three passages of Scripture. Do you see anything about us trying to win or overcome? No! Jesus already made us more than conquerors. Jesus already gave us the victory. Jesus always leads us in triumph. Why? *Jesus already won all of your battles!*

You don't have to battle; all you have to do is enjoy the victory! I don't battle; I just win. It is what I do and it is what Jesus made me to do. I win because Jesus won! When I begin to renew my mind to this wonderful truth, all the struggling to get free will stop and all the rejoicing that I am free will start. In Him, I always win; losing isn't possible when I am united with Christ.

Chapter 18

Hearing From God Is Normal

27 My sheep hear My voice, and I know them, and they follow Me.

John 10:27 NKJV

Jesus is the Shepherd and we are His sheep. Jesus said without hesitation that His sheep hear His voice; although, if you listened to most of the Church world, you would think the opposite. The majority of the Church thinks hearing from God is hard or abnormal. The reason most people think it's hard is because we haven't fully grasped the reality of being a spirit being united with God.

Remember what Jesus told Nicodemus? Jesus said that if you don't understand the basic truth of being a spirit being and being born again spiritually, you really can't understand any higher truths.

As a spirit being, it is normal to hear from God. Actually, as a spirit being, it should be more natural for us to hear from God than it is to hear a song on the radio. Why is that?

It's simple. You are a spirit and God is a spirit. You were born from the realm of the spirit; therefore, spiritual things should be more real to you than natural things. The problem is this truth isn't emphasized and 99.999% of people go through childhood being taught all about the natural realm and hardly anything about the spiritual realm. *Essentially, we are taught more about the world we are visiting than the world we are from; therefore, this natural world is more real to us.*

God is a spirit and therefore He will speak to us through spiritual means, not natural means. He isn't going to speak to your head; He is going to speak to your spirit. Your spirit, the real you, knows the voice of God. Your head may not realize it, but you do know the voice of God and it's normal to hear God speak.

1 Now Adam had sexual relations with his wife, Eve, and she became pregnant. When she gave birth to Cain, she said, "With the Lord's help, I have produced a man!" 2 Later she gave birth to his brother and named him Abel. When they grew up, Abel became a shepherd, while Cain cultivated the ground. 3 When it was time for the harvest, Cain presented some of his crops as a gift to the Lord. 4 Abel also brought a gift—the best portions of the firstborn lambs from his flock. The Lord accepted Abel and his gift, 5 but he did not accept Cain and his gift. This made Cain very angry, and he looked dejected. 6 "Why are you so angry?" the Lord asked Cain. "Why do you look so dejected? 7 You will be accepted if you do what is right. But if you refuse to do what is right, then watch out! Sin is crouching at the door, eager to control you. But you must subdue it and be its master." 8 One day Cain suggested to his brother, "Let's go out into the fields." And while they were in the field, Cain attacked his brother, Abel, and killed him. 9 Afterward the Lord asked Cain, "Where is your brother? Where is Abel?" "I don't know," Cain responded. "Am I my brother's guardian?" 10 But the Lord said, "What

have you done? Listen! Your brother's blood cries out to me from the ground! 11 Now you are cursed and banished from the ground, which has swallowed your brother's blood. 12 No longer will the ground yield good crops for you, no matter how hard you work! From now on you will be a homeless wanderer on the earth." 13 Cain replied to the Lord, "My punishment is too great for me to bear!

Genesis 4:1-13 NLT

There are several things I want you to see in this story of Cain and Abel. First of all, note that this story happened after Adam and Eve sinned, died spiritually and were kicked out of the Garden of Eden. Second, it's vitally important to understand that Cain and Abel were second generation sinners. They never walked and talked in the Garden with God like their parents. Taking into consideration this fact, notice that Cain not only heard God speak, but actually had a conversation with God – he heard God speaking entire sentences! Lastly, notice that Cain's conversation with God was after he killed Abel. Now let's put this all together. Cain, an unsaved murderer is having an effortless conversation with God!

As a Christian today, that should either tick you off or

seriously motivate you. After all, if an unsaved murderer can hear from God with ease, why shouldn't a born again, blood bought, spirit-filled child of God be able to hear God with ease? Do you know why Cain was able to hear God speak? It's actually very simple. First of all, Cain, even though he was unsaved, was still a spirit being. Secondly, it shows us that Adam and Even did a phenomenal job of teaching their children to hear God's voice.

Teaching Your Children

Adam and Eve didn't lead their children into a religion; they led them into a relationship with God to such a degree that hearing from God was normal – even as an unrighteous, unsaved being.

This shows us that as parents, we can and should teach our children to hear and recognize God's voice. It also shows us that hearing from God has more to do with our mind set than anything else. The issue, as with everything else spiritual, is our awareness. We don't have an equipment problem; we have an awareness problem.

The ability to hear from God isn't the issue because God is a spirit and we are a spirit; spirits can talk to and hear from spirits.

Here is something for you to think about. How many times have you felt unworthy or felt like you weren't good enough to hear from God? Do you realize it's not even a righteousness issue; it's not even a holiness issue. Cain proved you can be a murderer and still hear from God.

Hearing Satan Speak

Here is something else to think about. Have you ever heard Satan speak to you? Regardless of what kind of church you attend, you and I both know we have all had Satan talk to us and we heard him loud and clear. Remember the time he told you to lie to your boss? Remember when he was trying to get you to steal that money? Remember when he told you that person didn't deserve your forgiveness?

Yeah, we've all heard from the devil. Even people that aren't saved don't have a problem believing Satan is talking to people! However, you talk to most Christians about actually hearing God speak to them and they'll look at you like you lost your mind!

Do you know why you can hear Satan speak to you?

Because the idiot is a spirit too! Spirit beings can hear from other spirit beings just like a cow can hear from a cow and a horse can hear from a horse.

No, hearing from God should be the most normal and natural thing to the believer. Hearing from God should be more normal than hearing your best friend talk to you. Why? Because God is a spirit and you are a spirit and He lives within you by the Holy Spirit.

The Importance of Fellowship

If you really look at Jesus life and ministry, it's evident one of the main reasons for His success was not because of who He was, but because of what He knew. Jesus had fellowship with God. He spent time talking with God and hearing from God.

> **28 So Jesus said, "When you have lifted up the Son of Man on the cross, then you will understand that I am he. I do nothing on my own but say only what the Father taught me.**
>
> **John 8:28 NLT**

> **49 I don't speak on my own authority. The Father who sent me has commanded me what to say and how to**

say it. 50 And I know his commands lead to eternal
life; so I say whatever the Father tells me to say."

John 12:49-50 NLT

What if our fellowship with God was as important as Jesus fellowship with God? What if through that friendship, we got to the point that the only thing we said was what God told us. That would sure keep us out of a lot of trouble wouldn't it? It would also help us in doing the very works of Jesus!

If we are going to do what Jesus did, then we also need the same equipment. Not only do we have the same authority, the same power, the same spirit and the same righteousness, we also have the same ability to hear from God. If Jesus could hear from God, so can we with the very same clarity and ease.

Can you imagine the results we would get in life if we went into situations knowing exactly what God would say in those same situations? We would never make a mistake! We would always know exactly what to say and nail it every time. Do you realize this is possible?

If it doesn't sound realistic to you, it's because you are simply more aware of your natural limitations than your spiritual freedom in Christ. This is a spiritual reality here that you need to grab hold of and begin to pursue in your life!

I want you to understand this isn't anything you have to work to get good enough for nor is this something in which you have to put on some show to get to happen. If Cain the murderer could hear from God, you can certainly hear from God. If you can hear the devil speak to you (who is a spirit too), then you can also hear from God (who is a Spirit as well and is your Father).

If you can hear from God, you will be unstoppable in life.

Just like it's normal for you to talk to your parents, it's normal for you to talk to your Heavenly Father. You don't have to talk to Him in a low voice or in King James Version; talk to Him like your best friend AND expect to hear from Him as well – because that is normal. You need to start thinking like hearing from God is normal because it is.

The entire reason Cain conversed with God with ease was because he didn't know any better. Cain hadn't been to church so he could hear from the pastor that hearing from God was hard and abnormal. Cain hadn't attended Bible study enough to find out he wasn't spiritual enough to hang out with God. He certainly didn't get to attend a seminary where they taught him that God was too high and mysterious to even figure out.

Cain hadn't been indoctrinated with the goofy religion most of us have received; even after he murdered Abel, Cain didn't even act surprised to hear God speak.

Pray With Expectation To Hear

When you go to spend some time in prayer, go with the expectation to not only talk to God, but hear from God. This means you are not only going to have to start thinking this way, but you are also going to need to get your mind quiet so you can hear. The majority of our problem of hearing comes down to two issues: (1) not being aware that hearing from God is normal and (2) not getting our mind quiet.

Part of my daily routine in the mornings is my devotional time. I take the first few hours of my day to study and pray. I have some soft instrumental music I play the entire time that simply helps me to stay focused and keep my mind calm. I start out with a couple of devotionals that I read to simply get my mind on the things of God. I pray out of my mind for our country, our government, my church and the people and then I begin to pray in the Spirit.

Usually I start out with the purpose of simply building myself up and becoming more aware of Him and then I go into the direction of getting instruction and revelation from God. Depending on what day it is and what is going on, sometimes I need instruction as to how to handle a situation and sometimes it's regarding our vision and purpose as a ministry. Whatever the need may be, I always get an answer. It's not because I am something special and it's not because I am a minister; it is because I am a spirit being and God is my Father.

I always expect to hear from Him because I know His voice. Remember what Jesus said? "My sheep know my voice." That has been my confession for years and it is something we have instilled into my son Jake. Jake is going on seven years old right now and he firmly believes hearing from God is normal. Do you know why? Lacy and I have instilled that truth into him since he was a baby. Every day we have a confession we have him say that is filled with spiritual realities and one of them is "I know the voice of

God." It is a truth we were adamant would be instilled in Jake from a baby.

I knew that if Jake knew he could hear from God, he would be unstoppable in life. Even now when kids tell Jake he can't hear God, Jake is very adamant that he can – and it thrills my heart as a parent.

If You Can Hear From God, You've Got It Made

Think about that! If you can hear from God, you have it made. No problem can stump you. No situation can catch you off guard and you would never make a mistake. It's one of the greatest gifts God has given us and it has been one of the greatest battles Satan has waged against the Christian. If Satan can convince you hearing from God is hard and abnormal, you won't pursue it and if you won't pursue it, you'll never hear wisdom and revelation from Heaven.

Make this your confession and declare it every day: *Hearing from God is normal. Hearing from God is easy. Every time I pray, I hear God speak because I know His voice. I know even the tiniest whisper. I know God's leading and guidance. God speaks to my spirit and I hear Him every time. I am sensitive to the voice of God. I only say what He says. He is my Father and I am His child and it is normal for me to hear from my Dad.*

Chapter 19
Maintain The Connection

When you look at Jesus ministry, we find Him constantly talking about Who His Father was, where He was from and Who was working on the inside of Him. In essence, Jesus spent a great deal of time talking about His union and identification with God. If He was talking about it a lot, then we know Jesus was thinking about it a lot.

If you want the supernatural to be natural for you, you will have to maintain your connection. Remember what Jesus said about His relationship with the Father?

10 Do you not believe that I am in the Father, and the Father in Me? The words that I speak to you I do not speak on My own authority; but the Father who dwells in Me does the works.

John 14:10 NKJV

Don't think you will be any different than Jesus. If Jesus couldn't do anything on His own, you won't be able to do anything on your own either. This is why Jesus went on to tell us about the importance of our union with Him.

5 I am the vine, you are the branches. He who abides in Me, and I in him, bears much fruit; for without Me you can do nothing.

John 15:5 NKJV

Jesus wants to produce fruit through us and He made the fruit producing part easy; our responsibility is to maintain our connection by keeping our mind on Him. Just because we are connected to Jesus through our union doesn't mean we will automatically experience it.

Abiding In Him

The key is abiding; this means staying there and staying put. It means to dwell there, to live there and have our being there. Unfortunately, for most Christians, the only time we are abiding in Christ is on Sunday morning for about an hour. When we walk out the church door, our thoughts go back to our daily life and problems and we begin to abide outside of Christ once again. Then, we wonder why we don't experience fruit throughout the week, but the answer is simple: *What you abide in determines what you will experience; what you are connected to determines what will flow through you.*

Producing Fruit

In Mark 4, Jesus tells the parable of the sower. In this parable, we find some great truths about producing fruit and maintaining our thoughts and focus.

14 The sower sows the word. 15 And these are the ones by the wayside where the word is sown. When they hear, Satan comes immediately and takes away the word that was sown in their hearts. 16 These likewise are the ones sown on stony ground who, when they hear the word, immediately receive it with gladness; 17 and they have no root in themselves, and so endure only for a time. Afterward, when tribulation or persecution arises for the word's sake, immediately they stumble. 18 Now these are the ones sown among thorns; they are the ones who hear the word, 19 and the cares of this world, the deceitfulness of riches, and the desires for other things entering in choke the word, and it becomes unfruitful. 20 But these are the

**ones sown on good ground, those who hear the word,
accept it, and bear fruit: some thirtyfold, some sixty,
and some a hundred."**

Mark 4:14-20 NKJV

Satan is always after fruit; he is fine with the Word being sown as long as it doesn't produce fruit. Because he has no authority in our lives, the only thing Satan can do is endeavor to distract you and get your attention onto anything other than the realities of your union with Christ.

Notice that only one group of people produced fruit. The others didn't produce fruit because they were distracted and didn't maintain their connection. They all had the same equipment and the same ability to produce fruit, but they allowed the other things of life to hinder them.

This is why Satan daily bombards us with worries, cares, and concerns. It is why he constantly brings thoughts of lack and condemnation. Even though Jesus has unified us with Him, we can easily unplug from the Source of life when we take our mind off of Him.

**3 You will keep in perfect peace all who trust in you,
all whose thoughts are fixed on you!**

Isaiah 26:3 NLT

It is why we are told throughout the Bible to do something with our mind. If you want to experience peace in your mind and body, you have to fix your thoughts on Him. To fix your thoughts on Him means you put your thoughts there and leave them there; you put your thoughts on the realities of your union with Christ. If you want to be free of condemnation, keep your thoughts on Him. If you want to flow in the supernatural, you must fix your thoughts on Him.

When we trust in Him, that means we live our lives through Him and put our wisdom and abilities off to the side. It means we don't set aside the grace of God, but we allow our being to be through Him. We decrease in our lives so He can increase in our lives. The more He increases, the more peace and wholeness you experience - but it all starts with fixing your thoughts on Him and keeping them there.

If you can control your thoughts, you can control your destiny. If you can keep your mind connected to your union with Christ and abide in Him, you can keep the switch of faith on, the supernatural flowing in your life and bring peace into your life and others.

Three Practical Steps

I understand with our busy lives, this is a hard thing to do. When you have a family and kids, it makes it even harder! Everyone is competing for your time and focus, so it's important we take the necessary steps to keeping our awareness of God in our life.

1. Meditate on the Word. You don't have to read your Bible for five hours in order for it to do you any good. It's not about the quantity of time, but the quality of time. Many people focus on reading a certain number of chapters per day, but what good does it do you if you don't remember what you read? The best thing you can do is begin to read and when you get to a verse that really sticks out to you, stop reading. Then take that scripture and chew on it throughout the day. Think about it and meditate on it until you see something in it you never saw before. That is where faith comes because you allow the written Word to lead you into hearing the spoken Word which brings revelation.

2. Listen to good worship music. At my home, we always have worship music playing. It's important because not only does it help create a peaceful atmosphere in our home, but it helps to be a reminder to worship the Lord. I may be going about my chores at home not thinking about Him and yet as soon as I hear the music, it reminds me of Who is most important in my life. Many times I find Lacy or Jake singing or humming along with whatever is playing; it's just a natural thing that happens with music. As a parent, it's a great thing to hear your young child playing with his toys and singing unto God at the same time; it always puts a smile on mine and Lacy's face.

As you sing songs unto God, it will automatically put your thoughts on Him and it's also a great way to meditate on the Word of God. When the songs are actually Bible based and full of faith and truth, singing those Words from your mouth helps you not only keep your thoughts on Him, but also renew your mind to spiritual truths.

I must caution that you must be careful with the songs you sing. Just because it is labeled Christian doesn't mean the words are true. Just because it's on Christian radio doesn't mean it is of God. I've reached a point where I don't listen to much Christian music on the radio anymore. A lot of the music is filled with doubt, unbelief and doctrine based on experience instead of Scripture. Don't be singing stuff just because it's Christian and has a nice tune; check out the words and make sure it lines up with the Word. When you find some good music, begin to sing those wonderful songs of worship unto Him and watch what it does to your awareness of Him in your life.

3. Pray in tongues. I can't emphasize this one enough. Praying in tongues is one of the most beneficial things you can do to keep you thoughts focused on God and yet keep yourself charged up spiritually. The Bible says in 1 Corinthians 14:4 that when you speak in tongues, you edify yourself. The word *edify* means "to charge up like a battery." When you pray in tongues, the Holy Spirit is giving you the words and so you are working together. This causes you to become very aware of His presence and the result is you will become much more aware of spiritual things.

I pray in tongues all the time - when I'm driving, cutting grass, pushing the shopping cart...it doesn't matter. It is of utmost priority that I maintain my awareness of God in my life. Now when I am in public, I keep it quiet; you don't go around making a scene and scaring people. However, even in the busy times of our day, we can still take advantage of this God given gift of keeping our thoughts on Him. Speaking in tongues is a wonderful by-product of the Baptism of the Holy Spirit that God has given us; it is necessary for us to take advantage of it if we want the supernatural to be natural in our lives.

Chapter 20

Ready For Every Occasion

If you want to see the supernatural, you have to be ready for every occasion that presents itself. Jesus always maintained His connection with God; therefore, He was always ready for opportunities that needed a touch of the supernatural.

11 Now it happened, the day after, that He went into a city called Nain; and many of His disciples went with Him, and a large crowd. 12 And when He came near the gate of the city, behold, a dead man was being carried out, the only son of his mother; and she was a widow. And a large crowd from the city was with her. 13 When the Lord saw her, He had compassion on her

and said to her, "Do not weep." 14 Then He came and touched the open coffin, and those who carried him stood still. And He said, "Young man, I say to you, arise." 15 So he who was dead sat up and began to speak. And He presented him to his mother.

Luke 7:11-15 NKJV

When Jesus went to the city of Nain, we have no information given to us that would lead us to believe Jesus knew ahead of time that a funeral was taking place. Instead, what we see is Jesus going into Nain and He stumbles upon a funeral.

The sky didn't open up and a host of angels begin to sing. We don't see Jesus start to shake and tremble under the power of God. We see nothing spectacular happen here showing either Jesus knowing about this event ahead of time nor Jesus experiencing anything naturally at the event. What we see is a supernatural Jesus, connected to God and at the sight of the woman's grief, the compassion of God begins to flow through Jesus.

We see the supernatural simply a natural process in Jesus; compassion flowed and Jesus moved. Notice Jesus command – very simple, to the point and effective. Jesus authoritatively said, "Young man, I say to you arise." There was no big scene, no entertainment, no hammond B3 blaring in the background, no lights, no smoke and no music; it was simply Jesus being who He was. Jesus didn't have to put on anything or try to do something; Jesus simply was who He was: a supernatural being. When you know who you are, you don't have to try and be something you're not.

People Need You When They Need You

Standing at a funeral procession is not the time to try and believe you receive; it's not the time you try and get spiritual. There will be many situations presented to you where people don't have time for you to "feel" spiritual. They won't have time for you to fast and pray for twenty one days so you can hear God and feel God. Life or death situations will not wait on you to get spiritual enough! This is why you need to maintain your connection with God. This is why you need to be able to move based on what you know, not what you feel.

It's interesting to me that the majority of healings that took place with Jesus didn't happen because Jesus went looking for them; they happened because they were presented to Jesus as He was simply going about His day.

Most Christians today, if presented with a random situation, would walk away from the possibility of a miracle because they didn't feel ready. *If you are being led by your feelings, you will never feel ready.* However, even if your body is saying it's tired and your emotions are telling you they don't feel like working a miracle, you can by faith act on what you know. If you'll look to the Holy Spirit, He will always show you what to do in the situation allowing you to bypass your feelings.

1 On the third day there was a wedding in Cana of Galilee, and the mother of Jesus was there. 2 Now both Jesus and His disciples were invited to the wedding. 3 And when they ran out of wine, the mother of Jesus said to Him, "They have no wine." 4 Jesus said to her, "Woman, what does your concern have to do with Me? My hour has not yet come." 5 His mother said to the servants, "Whatever He says to you, do it." 6 Now there were set there six waterpots of stone, according to the manner of purification of the Jews, containing twenty or thirty gallons apiece. 7 Jesus said to them, "Fill the waterpots with water." And they filled them

up to the brim. 8 And He said to them, "Draw some out now, and take it to the master of the feast." And they took it. 9 When the master of the feast had tasted the water that was made wine, and did not know where it came from (but the servants who had drawn the water knew), the master of the feast called the bridegroom. 10 And he said to him, "Every man at the beginning sets out the good wine, and when the guests have well drunk, then the inferior. You have kept the good wine until now!"

John 2:1-10 NKJV

In John 2, we find Jesus not on a ministry trip, not preaching in a church service, but at a party. Jesus wasn't at the party to do ministry; Jesus was there to enjoy the wedding. During the wedding reception, Mary tells Jesus she is out of wine, to which Jesus replies, "And how does that concern me?" It appears Mary was the wedding coordinator or at the very least, responsible for the reception.

Well, she doesn't take Jesus answer too seriously because she turns to her servants and says, "Do whatever Jesus tells you to do." Basically, Mary put a demand on Jesus to manifest the supernatural and yet Jesus wasn't there to do that; Jesus was there to party!

Despite what seemed to be a lack of preparation, we know Jesus was already prepared because He always maintained His connection to God. Many times throughout the Gospels, we find Jesus withdrawing from the crowds to spend time in prayer and fellowship with the Father. Jesus many times spoke of His union with the Father and dependence on the Father. His fellowship and union with God was obviously always on His mind.

In one of the most "unsupernatural" of situations, Jesus manifested the supernatural in a very natural way. Jesus bypassed His feelings, bypassed the environment and produced the miraculous. Just like in the other situations, you don't see Jesus trying to work up something so He could feel supernatural or to try and get God to do something. Simply because Jesus knew who He was and what He possessed, He naturally responded from His union with God.

1 Now Peter and John went up together to the temple at the hour of prayer, the ninth hour. 2 And a certain man lame from his mother's womb was carried, whom they laid daily at the gate of the temple which is called Beautiful, to ask alms from those who entered the temple; 3 who, seeing Peter and John about to go into

the temple, asked for alms. 4 And fixing his eyes on him, with John, Peter said, "Look at us." 5 So he gave them his attention, expecting to receive something from them. 6 Then Peter said, "Silver and gold I do not have, but what I do have I give you: In the name of Jesus Christ of Nazareth, rise up and walk." 7 And he took him by the right hand and lifted him up, and immediately his feet and ankle bones received strength. 8 So he, leaping up, stood and walked and entered the temple with them—walking, leaping, and praising God.

Acts 3:1-8 NKJV

This is a lot like the miracles of Jesus in that Peter and John weren't going somewhere with the intention of manifesting the supernatural. Peter and John were simply going to the temple to pray when the lame man at the gate stopped them. Even in this, the lame man didn't ask for healing; he simply asked for some money. Even though Peter and John weren't going with the intention of working the miraculous, because they knew who they were and what they possessed, they were still ready for a supernatural opportunity.

Peter said, "What I do have I will give to you!" If you

know you have something, you don't have to depend on feelings. If I have my keys in my hand, I don't have to depend on my emotions, feelings and circumstances in order to give away what is in my hand.

Peter knew what he had and he gave it away. He knew he had the power of God at his disposal, so Peter released that power into the lame man and made a miracle happen! Just like with Samson, you don't need to have a feeling to move; *all you need is a knowing!* When you know, it will flow and it will flow very naturally.

The Blind Woman

I'll never forget Sunday, November 5, 2006. At the end of the service, I had a word of knowledge about someone who had just received a bad doctor's report. A woman came up and told me she had received a bad report about her heart and it would require surgery. After I ministered to her, I asked if there was anyone else that needed healing. Several people came up to the front and I began to pray for them.

The last person in the line was a short elderly woman. I walked up to her and asked, "What can I do for you?" She responded, "I'm blind." I said, "What do you mean blind?" and she said, "Pastor Chad, I can't see."

Honestly, it shook me to the core. I had never prayed for a blind person and the thoughts of doubt started bombarding me. At this point in ministry, we were just getting started and taking our first steps toward a ministry of the supernatural.

As I looked at this blind woman, I grabbed hold of my emotions, my feelings and my thoughts and subdued them. I began to think about my union with Christ and the authority of which I had. All of a sudden, a confidence like I had never known hit me – I knew that I knew that I knew this woman was going to walk out completely healed.

This knowing that came upon me was the Holy Spirit manifesting the gift of faith. I couldn't tell you how I knew, but I knew she was going to be healed. (As a side note, let me add that I was very new to this and God was helping me out because I was just getting started. This was one of the few times where God gave me a jump start before I said or did anything. Now it usually takes me stepping out quite a few steps in faith before I begin to see the gifts of the Spirit in operation. It is simply because God expects us to mature and as we mature, He expects more of us.)

So, I stepped out on what I knew and told everyone she

was blind, but that she was going to walk out of the building seeing! I then put my hands on her eyes and commanded them to be whole. I stepped back and said, "Mam, tell me what you see." She said, "Well, I can barely see you, but it's very blurry and mostly gray." Well, that information got me excited because she was actually seeing something and with that, it also got the congregation excited.

I put my hands on her again and put more anointing in those eyes. I stepped back and said, "Mam, what can you see?" She said, "Well, now I can see the outline of your tie, but I can't make out the details." So with the second time of putting my hands on her eyes, she was seeing even better. Then I said, "Alright everyone. This is the last time I'm going to lay hands on her and this time, we are going to finish this thing and get perfect results."

I put my hands on her eyes one more time then stepped back and said, "Mam, tell me what you see." The elderly woman said, "I can see every perfectly!" I'm not sure what happened at that moment because I was so excited, I took off running around the sanctuary! I think it would suffice to say the church went crazy at that moment.

That was the first major miracle in our ministry and it

happened at a moment that I was not feeling very spiritual at all. I had just gotten through praying for people with some minor ailments and then comes the blind lady. The problem was I didn't think I was ready to take on blind people yet; however, I had been preparing myself for about two years meditating on the truths we are looking at in this book.

When my feelings tried to discourage me and take me away from a miracle, I was able to fall back to what I knew to be true: Jesus was the Vine and I was the branch. Whatever was flowing through Him was flowing through me and therefore, there was no lack or insufficiency keeping me from getting the job done.

Chapter 21
Jesus Wasn't Weird

23 Now when He was in Jerusalem at the Passover, during the feast, many believed in His name when they saw the signs which He did.

John 2:23 NKJV

There are a number of churches and ministries out there who are hungry for the supernatural and for that I am grateful. Most of our churches today are just dead. There are no moves of God, no miracles, no manifestations of the Spirit and really no ministry going on. The only difference between most churches and a funeral home is a casket. Put a casket in most churches and you could label it a funeral home because there is no life there.

Fortunately, we do have some who are seeking the supernatural, but when you don't have a foundation of the Word under you, the result is that people get weird. This is why so much of the world and Christiandom wants nothing to do with the spirit-filled Charismatic folks.

I'll be honest, I've grown up in what we call the Charismatic circles and I have experienced lots of weird stuff; it's probably why I so much seek to produce the supernatural without all of the fluff. When I get weirded out in a church service, it's pretty bad!

Square Dancing and Barking Dogs

I remember one time I was in a church that was holding some revival type services. Now I have to give credit to this church because they were hungry and seeking after the supernatural. The problem was they had a ton of zeal and almost zero Word; the result was a fiasco.

I remember Lacy went with me and we weren't even fifteen minutes into the service when Lacy looked at me and said, "This is getting ridiculous; can we please go?" I have to admit I was ready to go because I was somewhat grieved in my spirit, but on the natural side of things, I was trying not to laugh hysterically. During the worship, there were groups of people up in the front square dancing;

another man was literally humping a woman by the wall and another man was barking like a dog. I wasn't sure whether to laugh or cry!

I couldn't help but wonder what someone totally unchurched would think in seeing this. Was this something that would draw people unto Jesus? I don't think so.

Things Of The Spirit Draw People Unto Jesus

A lot of the things we experience in services that we label as a move of the Holy Spirit, I would be inclined to label a move of our flesh. There are a lot of things that have gone on in Charismatic circles that we've called supernatural, but in reality, were totally natural. I've found this to be true: when the Holy Spirit is really behind something, it will draw people unto Jesus, not cause them to run scared out the back door.

I've read the Gospels numerous times and not once have I found where Jesus acted weird. Jesus was naturally supernatural. He didn't put on the entertainment that we see in Charismatic circles today. Jesus didn't try to make something happen that wasn't there. He flawlessly and naturally flowed with the Holy Spirit and His union with God. When Jesus prayed for the sick, people didn't get scared and weirded out. When Jesus manifested the power of God, the crowds didn't start looking for the exit doors. No, when Jesus manifested the supernatural, it caused the people to praise God!

1 When the Day of Pentecost had fully come, they were all with one accord in one place. 2 And suddenly there came a sound from heaven, as of a rushing mighty wind, and it filled the whole house where they were sitting. 3 Then there appeared to them divided tongues, as of fire, and one sat upon each of them. 4 And they were all filled with the Holy Spirit and began to speak with other tongues, as the Spirit gave them utterance. 5 And there were dwelling in Jerusalem Jews, devout men, from every nation under heaven. 6 And when this sound occurred, the multitude came together, and were confused, because everyone heard them speak in his own language. 7 Then they were all amazed and marveled, saying to one another, "Look, are not all these who speak Galileans? 8 And how is it that we hear, each in our own language in which we were born? 9 Parthians and Medes and Elamites, those dwelling in Mesopotamia, Judea

and Cappadocia, Pontus and Asia, 10 Phrygia and Pamphylia, Egypt and the parts of Libya adjoining Cyrene, visitors from Rome, both Jews and proselytes, 11 Cretans and Arabs—we hear them speaking in our own tongues the wonderful works of God." 12 So they were all amazed and perplexed, saying to one another, "Whatever could this mean?" 13 Others mocking said, "They are full of new wine." 14 But Peter, standing up with the eleven, raised his voice and said to them, "Men of Judea and all who dwell in Jerusalem, let this be known to you, and heed my words. 15 For these are not drunk, as you suppose, since it is only the third hour of the day.

Acts 2:1-15 NKJV

One hundred twenty people were filled with the Holy Spirit and began speaking in tongues. What started out in the upper room spilled out onto the streets. When the crowds on the street heard the disciples speaking in various languages which they understood, they thought they were drunk.

What's interesting to me is that the people didn't run away scared and didn't necessarily think they were weird either. I believe many of us spirit-filled Charismatic people may have added to the word *drunk*. There are a lot of activities that go on in our churches under the classification of "drunk in the spirit" that I often wonder if it's really of the Spirit. Remember, anything that is of the Holy Spirit will draw people unto Jesus. Much of what I have seen classified as "drunk in the spirit" has caused lots and lots of people to run scared out of church and never wanting to go back because of what they experienced.

However, look at what happened when the one hundred twenty disciples were "drunk" in the spirit? Three thousand people accepted Jesus as their Lord and Savior! When is the last time you saw thousands come to Jesus because of modern day "drunk in the spirit" Christians? If people are running away from the church instead of running to Jesus, you have to ask yourself, "Is this really by the influence of the Holy Spirit?"

Granted, I appreciate a mighty zeal for God and I know we are all growing in the things of the spirit. I also know that revelation is progressive and there are things we understand a great deal better than we did thirty and forty years ago. Yet, if we want to progress in the supernatural, it means we must also work on weeding out the flesh so we can experience more of the spirit.

It's like John the Baptist said, "I must decrease so Jesus can increase." The more we grow in our union with Christ, the more of Him that will flow and the less of us that will be in the way. Our goal should be to fully experience the truth Paul stated to the church of Galatia.

20 I have been crucified with Christ; It is no longer I who live but Christ lives in me.
                                                Galatians 2:20 NKJV

When we live like this, we will experience the unadulterated, unfiltered, one hundred proof supernatural manifestations of the power of God and it will cause people at the very least to consider the reality of God.

Chapter 22
Signs

A major problem with most Christians today is that we don't know we have anything to give away. It is why we sit around twiddling our thumbs waiting on God to do something; we pray for moves of God and wonder why nothing is happening.

Do you know why most of the Church today isn't experiencing the supernatural power of God? I'll tell you: we are waiting on a move instead of realizing we are a move. If you want to see God move, then get up and MOVE!

You have God on the inside of you! You have His life on the inside of you! You have the Dispenser of the gifts on the inside of you. The reason why God gave us all of this is not only so we can live in victory, but also so God can use us to give the world signs of His presence!

If we don't release the life of God to the world, who will? If the world can't experience God through the Church, how else are they supposed to experience Him?

As a result of the lack of power in the Church today, most churches have resorted to programs to help fill the void. We boast about our food pantries, shelters, business schools and other social service programs as to why we are a success for Jesus. Social service programs are great, but they can't be a substitute for the power of God in churches.

Yes, Jesus provided money for the poor and food for those who were hungry, but do you realize that anyone can do that? You don't have to be saved to do those things; you don't need the supernatural to give the poor some money, food, or clothes.

Jesus went about teaching, preaching and healing. Most of our churches are doing the first two and think they are doing effective ministry. You can't do effective ministry without signs and wonders! Teaching and preaching are needed, but if the Word preached isn't manifested, then how is it any different to the unbeliever than a good speech?

Jesus didn't teach his followers to be social workers; He taught them how to be miracle workers. Why? Miracles are the proof that God is real. Miracles are signs for the unbeliever to show them God is real and they are a wake up call to the believer who has become calloused to the things of God.

19 They were convinced by the power of miraculous signs and wonders and by the power of God's Spirit. In this way, I have fully presented the Good News of Christ from Jerusalem all the way to Illyricum.

Romans 15:19 NLT

Based on this scripture, are our churches fully presenting the good news of Christ? If not, it's high time we get going because the world is waiting. In the same manner as Jesus, the apostle Paul based his ministry on the manifestation of the Word of God.

37 If I do not do the works of My Father, do not believe Me; 38 but if I do, though you do not believe Me, believe the works, that you may know and believe that the Father is in Me, and I in Him.

John 10:36-38 NLT

The modern Church has taken the importance of signs and cast them off as unnecessary and unneeded. Many denominations don't even believe in miracles anymore and state they were only for the early Church, but it's interesting to me that Jesus thought they were important for everyone!

People may try to argue about doctrine with you, but it's hard to debate someone rising from the dead, a paralyzed person getting out of a wheelchair or a blind person being healed! A man with an experience is never at the mercy of a man with an argument.

The power of God is needed today more than ever before – especially in the Church. We are living in a day in which the Church is rapidly slipping away from the truths of God's Word and it will take the supernatural to awaken the Church and get it headed back in the right direction.

> **A man with an experience is never at the mercy of a man with an argument.**

God wants to manifest Himself through signs, wonders and miracles because He doesn't want anyone to die and go to Hell. God wants everyone to be saved and it is why we must understand who we are and the supernatural power of God that can flow through us if we will allow it.

15 And He said to them, "Go into all the world and preach the gospel to every creature. 16 He who believes and is baptized will be saved; but he who does not believe will be condemned. 17 And these signs will follow those who believe: In My name they will cast out demons; they will speak with new tongues; 18 they will take up serpents; and if they drink anything deadly, it will by no means hurt them; they will lay hands on the sick, and they will recover." 19 So then, after the Lord had spoken to them, He was received up into heaven, and sat down at the right hand of God. 20 And they went out and preached everywhere, the Lord working with them and confirming the word through the accompanying signs. Amen.

Mark 16:15-20 NKJV

The word *signs* comes from the Greek word *semeion* which means "a sign, mark or token by which God authenticates the men sent by him, or by which men prove that the cause they are pleading is God's." This word was used to describe the signature of a seal applied to a document to guarantee its authenticity.[1]

In Mark 16, Jesus gives the Great Commission and is sending His disciples into the world to preach the Gospel. As He sent them forth, Jesus said God's seal would be upon the message so the world would know not only were the disciples sent by God, but also the message was true.

The disciples didn't have to try and work something up or follow a formula to try and have signs, wonders and miracles; all they had to do was walk in their union with Christ. Mark 16:20 says the Lord was working with them and confirming the Word. In the same way the Father was working through Jesus and supernaturally confirming the Word with miracles and signs of authenticity, Jesus will do the same thing through you and I.

Miracles should be normal for the believer. The supernatural should be natural for the believer. The miracle realm should be our normal realm; it should be the realm we live, move and have our being in because we live, move and have our being through Christ.

6 As you therefore have received Christ Jesus the Lord, so walk in Him.

Colossians 2:6 NKJV

Friend, if you have received the Anointed One and His

anointing, it is time we begin to walk in the Anointed One and His anointing and allow the supernatural to be natural for us. There is a world that is waiting on the supernatural sons of God to reveal themselves. There is a body of believers called the Church that is in dire need of a few people to begin fanning the flames of revival one last time.

Don't ever underestimate the worlds' hunger for the power of God. They aren't turned off by the supernatural; they are turned off by the fake cover ups. Let them experience the real and they will thank you for eternity. There should be so many divine interventions in our life that it causes the world to take notice!

God put you and I on this earth at this very time for such a time as this. It is our time to live the supernatural life God intended from the beginning of time - a life where we walk with God, talk with God and manifest God all throughout the earth with the utmost of ease.

If you have received Christ as your Lord, let us today begin to walk in Him and live through Him and have our being in Him. Let us stay connected to the Vine and let His power and life unconsciously flow through us. Let us forever be aware that Christ lives in us and the life we live, we live by faith in Him allowing the supernatural to flow through us as naturally as we breathe.

Evidence Of The Supernatural

This is the deaf woman from Walmart that was healed during a Sunday morning service in Texas. Here she is pictured with Chad Gonzales and the one hundred dollars he bet her that God would heal her if she came to church on Sunday. God instantly healed her and she still was blessed with the one hundred dollars.

This young girl was born with a short leg. During a youth conference in Spokane, Washington, God instantly grew her leg out.

Here is the same girl from the picture above after God grew out her right leg. She is holding the shoes she wore during the conference; as you can see, her right shoe had a lift built into it. The following week, her pastors presented her with a new pair of shoes.

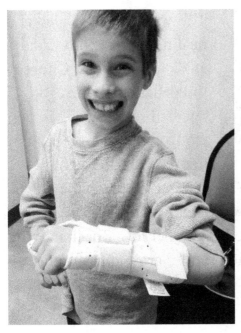

This young boy had a broken wrist. He and his mother attended a healing conference with Chad Gonzales at Trinity Church in Jonesboro, Arkansas. During the service, God healed his wrist without anyone touching Him but Jesus. The mother stated they watched the swelling and bruising go away while simply sitting in the service.

Here is a picture of him the next day riding his bike - without any brace on his arm!

This woman was healed at a healing service with Chad at Victorious Faith Church in Portland City, Oregon. She had serious back issues, along with lack of feeling in her thighs. After being ministered to, all the feeling came back in her legs. She said she felt something in her lower back moving and adjusting itself. She then moved around freely and even danced a little jig!

This woman was also healed at a healing service with Chad in Portland, Oregon. She had multiple issues in her body in which she was instantly healed. Her right leg was short and grew out. Her right ankle, which was fused, regained all movement. She also had a lump on her chest that dissolved during the service.

Prayer For Salvation And
The Baptism Of The Holy Spirit

Dear friend, it is the desire of God that everyone accepts His free gift of salvation. God sent the greatest gift Heaven had so the world could be set free; that precious gift was Jesus! Despite knowing the mistakes you would make, He died for you anyway. Jesus knew the mistakes you would make, yet He still climbed up on the cross. Why? His love was greater than your sin.

Romans 10:9-10 says if you will confess Jesus as your Lord and Savior and believe that He arose from the dead, you will be saved. You see, salvation has nothing to do with works. It doesn't matter what church you belong to, how many little old ladies you help across the street or how much you give the church. You cannot earn salvation; you cannot buy salvation; you must simply accept salvation.

Another free gift that God has provided is the Baptism of the Holy Spirit. In Acts 2, we find the Baptism of the Holy Spirit being given to the Church. God desires that you be filled with His Spirit with the evidence of speaking in tongues.

God said in Acts 2:38 that this life changing gift was for everyone, not just a select few. It wasn't just for those living in Bible days; it was given to everyone who would accept Jesus as Lord and Savior. Jesus said the purpose of the Baptism of the Holy Spirit was so you could be a witness! You'll find that when you receive the Baptism of the Holy Spirit, it allows you to operate in the fullness of God's power and be a blessing to the entire world. Essentially, you could say that salvation gets you into a relationship with God and the Baptism of the Holy Spirit helps you get others into a relationship with God.

Regardless of who you are, God has a plan for your life. He wants you to be successful, have all your needs met and live a life of victory. God wants every day of your life to be a day full of peace and joy, but it all begins with Jesus being your Lord and Savior. If you have never accepted Jesus as your Lord and Savior, please pray this prayer with me right now:

Jesus, I confess that I am a sinner. I realize I can't do this on my own. I believe with my heart and confess with my mouth that you died on the cross for my sins and sicknesses and arose from the dead. I ask you to be the Lord and Savior of my life. I thank you for forgiving me of my sins and loving me enough to give your life for me. I thank you that I am now a child of God! I now ask you for the Baptism of the Holy Spirit. You said in Your Word that it was a free gift so I receive it now. I thank you for my Heavenly prayer language!

We encourage you to become involved in a solid Bible based church. If you need help finding a church in your area, contact us through the information below.

Begin reading your Bible and praying in the Spirit daily. Now it is time to start developing your relationship with your Heavenly Father and growing in the Lord - and don't forget to tell someone about what Jesus did for you! Remember that God is good and He has good things in store for you!

If you prayed this prayer, would like assistance in locating a local church or this book has impacted your life, we would love to hear from you! You can also obtain a full listing of our books and other teaching materials by contacting us at:

www.ChadGonzales.com

About The Author

Chad and Lacy Gonzales are graduates of Rhema Bible Training College. Chad also holds a M.Ed. in Counseling from Lamar University.

With an emphasis on one's identity in Christ, Chad and Lacy bring a powerful and practical message of faith and grace to the world. The ministry God has called them to is one filled with signs, wonders and miracles. Declaring the Gospel with boldness and without compromise, mighty miracles of healing are common in their meetings.

Bibliography

Chapter One

1. "Incorruptible" Strong's Exhaustive Concordance: King James Bible. Updated ed. La Habra: Lockman Foundation, 1995. Bible Study Tools Online. Web. May 2015.

2. Nosson Scherman. The Chumash: The Stone Edition, Full Size (ArtScroll) (English and Hebrew Edition) The Torah: Haftaros and Five Megillos with a Commentary Anthologized from the Rabbinic Writings Mesorah Pubns Ltd. June 1, 1993

3. "Fruit." Strong's Exhaustive Concordance: King James Bible. Updated ed. La Habra: Lockman Foundation, 1995. Bible Study Tools Online. Web. May 2015.

Chapter Eight

1. "Life." Strong's Exhaustive Concordance: King James Bible. Updated ed. La Habra: Lockman Foundation, 1995. Bible Study Tools Online. Web. May 2015.

2. Renner, Rick. *Sparkling Gems From The Greek.* Teach All Nations. 2003.

Chapter 22

1. Renner, Rick. *Sparkling Gems From The Greek.* Teach All Nations. 2003.

CPSIA information can be obtained
at www.ICGtesting.com
Printed in the USA
LVHW020312270523
748222LV00008B/339